BIRDS OF THE TRANS-PECOS

Number Thirty-Seven

The Corrie Herring Hooks Series

BIRDS
OF THE **TRANS-PECOS**

Jim Peterson
and Barry R. Zimmer

Foreword by Victor Emanuel

Drawings by Gail Diane Yovanovich

 UNIVERSITY OF TEXAS PRESS, AUSTIN

Dedicated to the Pioneers of Trans-Pecos Ornithology

Josselyn Van Tyne, Lena McBee, Mary Belle Keefer, Frances Williams, George M. Sutton, Pansy Espy, Clay and Jodie Miller

LIBRARY OF CONGRESS
CATALOGING-IN-PUBLICATION DATA

Peterson, Jim, 1952–
Birds of the Trans-Pecos / Jim Peterson and Barry Zimmer ; foreword by Victor Emanuel ; drawings by Gail Diane Yovanovich.   p.   cm. — (Corrie Herring Hooks series ; no. 37) Includes bibliographical references and index.
ISBN 0-292-76583-5 (alk. paper). —ISBN 0-292-76584-3 (pbk. : alk. paper)
1. Birds—Texas. 2. Birds—Trans-Pecos (Tex. and N.M.)
I. Zimmer, Barry. II. Title. III. Series.
QL684.T4P38   1998
598'.09764'9—dc21   98-25747

CONTENTS

ILLUSTRATIONS AND TABLES

DRAWINGS

PHOTOGRAPHS *(following p. 80)*

MAPS

TABLES

FOREWORD

THE TRANS-PECOS region of West Texas has long attracted the interest of naturalists and birders. It is a vast and varied landscape composed of many habitats—grassland, desert, riparian areas, and mountains. Larger than several states, its bird list is longer than all but four states'. This excellent book provides a much-needed overview of the bird life of this fascinating region.

Barry Zimmer and Jim Peterson have both made important contributions to our knowledge of Trans-Pecos bird life. They are well qualified to write about the birds of the Trans-Pecos. Much, however, remains to be learned, and this book will provide a starting point for further exploration.

Many people think of Texas as an endless flat landscape with little variety. Much of Texas is flat, but its eight major biogeographic regions each possess a very distinctive assemblage of flora and fauna. The Trans-Pecos is the most scenic of these regions and in many ways the most interesting for naturalists. Mountains that are "Mexican" biologically reach the United States only in the Trans-Pecos, southern New Mexico, and southern Arizona. In these mountains, altitudinal zonation produces a much higher degree of diversity than in similar mountains further north. This results in a rich assemblage of birds, some of which center their North American distribution here. The most striking example is the Colima

Warbler, whose entire North American range is confined to a few hundred acres in the Chisos Mountains of the Big Bend country, one of the smallest breeding ranges of any North American bird.

The Trans-Pecos is a major migration pathway and important wintering area for many birds. As the region has become better known, a number of exciting vagrants have been discovered, including several that had never been seen in the United States. Where else in the world could one find a Red-necked Stint in August only 10 miles from the site where a Gray Silky-flycatcher was discovered one winter?

The Trans-Pecos is one of the most exciting birding areas in North America. It is a land with a rich history, great vistas, few people, starry skies, and marvelous birds. It has hot deserts, cool mountains, desert oases, birdy reservoirs, a fascinating plant community, and great wildflowers. Its long border with Mexico and its Mexican character make it an exotic and alluring land of diverse cultures and landscapes, and great bird diversity.

Whether you are hiking a mountain trail in the Chisos looking out over the expanses of northern Mexico, birding a cottonwood grove by the Rio Grande that is alive with birds, or checking out a lake or reservoir, the Trans-Pecos will provide you with great birding and wonderful experiences. For many years it has been my favorite birding area in Texas. With the publication of *Birds of the Trans-Pecos*, we can all enjoy the birds of this region with greater knowledge and understanding.

Victor Emanuel

PREFACE

AT THIS WRITING, 483 bird species have been recorded in the Trans-Pecos area defined in this book. The very first draft of this manuscript showed 472 total species. Several additions and a few American Ornithologists' Union (A.O.U.) species splits have created the current number. At this rate, approximately one species is added to the Trans-Pecos species list per year.

The task of creating a book (and an accurate database) on the birds of the Trans-Pecos was daunting for several reasons. The major difficulty was not just the size of the area (approximating the size of South Carolina) but its remote nature coupled with the low population density. Jeff Davis County, for example, has nearly as many square miles as the state of Connecticut, but a population so small that it might fit comfortably in a large Dallas apartment complex. Published bird sightings were thin and ornithological surveys were largely unknown.

Since the mid-1970's, the documentation of bird records in Texas has been more thoroughly scrutinized and increasingly well maintained. Bird observation and record keeping in the Trans-Pecos began with the pioneers to whom we dedicated this book. At that time, the birding network was a small group of people who were vocal enough to make their sightings known to others outside of the area. Their work led to a few journal publications on the area's avifauna, many of these writings dating to the early 1900's. Included in those early decades were reports from several great ornithologists such as Louis Agassiz Fuertes and George Miksch Sutton. Most reports, however, came from the early residents. Some were ranchers and some were city dwellers. Many were women.

Beginning in 1973, however, bird observations in the Trans-Pecos began to be published for popular consumption. Roland H. Wauer began the process with his work *A Field Guide to the Birds of the Big Bend* (1973). Concurrent with the publication of Wauer's book was the extraordinary research that resulted in *The Bird Life of Texas* by Oberholser and Kincaid (1974). To this day, *The Bird Life of Texas* is a barometer by which all other documentation of Texas ornithology is measured.

These publications were followed by three events that aided the process by which unusual bird sightings are reviewed in Texas. The first was the formation in 1976 of the Texas Bird Records Committee (TBRC), a standing committee of the Texas Ornithological Society. This reviewing committee helped establish a process of evaluation for bird rarities and created an official checklist of Texas birds.

The second event was the Texas Breeding Bird Atlas Project (as yet unpublished). The research for this project began in 1987 and was completed in 1992. The TBBAP, like many atlas projects before it, created criteria to measure a bird's potential as a breeding species. Observers were in the field for the specific reason of collecting bird data, and the amount of information generated during that period added immeasurably to our knowledge of the Trans-Pecos avifauna.

Finally, the advent of the Internet has created new standards in the processing of information. A bird sighting is now minutes from every interested individual. Follow-up times for rare bird confirmation may now be hours instead of days. Pictures and drawings can be transmitted through cyberspace, and the reviewing process itself is reduced exponentially.

However, because of the small number of people living in the Trans-Pecos, bird reports from this area are still quite thin. Based on the number of observers in the field, it remains, by far, the most poorly covered area in the state. Without computer capabilities, reports of an unusual bird by a single observer may take two to three days for confirmation. Sightings by a knowledgeable landowner may go into a personal journal, but never receive adequate follow-up. Observations by someone visiting from out of state may follow that observer back home, but never find their way into the state's bird database.

I accomplished this very feat in 1981, when I observed a Bridled Titmouse in the Basin area of Big Bend National Park. Not knowing it was a TBRC "review" species for the state, I simply recorded it in my notes and, after a lengthy stay in the Southwest, returned to my home in Connecticut. After moving to Texas in 1986, I quickly discovered how important this record could have been. It is a species for which, at this writing, there is still not an accepted record for the state of Texas. I thought about submitting the sighting six years later, but it would have been a single sighting by a single observer submitted six years after the fact. By my own current standards, this record could not even make the list in this very manuscript except as "hypothetical."

The big picture of the Trans-Pecos avifauna is still far from clear. Ornithological information from the area remains only a trickle compared to almost any other area of the United States. In particular, very few observations come from the Trans-Pecos mountain ranges. The collected data at these high-elevation locations have only recently moved beyond the "pioneer" stages. Furthermore, habitat changes, air quality standards, and water resource issues still pose serious questions for the area's wildlife. In many ways, the Trans-Pecos is only now beginning to yield the kind of information that will allow the appropriate use and management of one of the most uniquely diverse and scenic areas of Texas.

Jim Peterson, 1997

ACKNOWLEDGMENTS

Needless to say, several people have contributed to this massive database of Trans-Pecos bird records. However, the single most important person in regard to all Texas bird records is Greg Lasley. Without his tireless work as secretary of the Texas Bird Records Committee, many of these Trans-Pecos records would be suspect. His additions to this manuscript were many, and his eye for detail was greatly appreciated.

We are also appreciative of the drawings of Gail Yovanovich, whose work we have always admired. Her art adds spice to this sometimes dry subject matter, and many of her works can be used as educational aids in the field.

Other contributors include Ro Wauer, Kelly Bryan, Brian Gibbons, Victor Emanuel, David Riskind (who contributed nearly the entire section on "Grasslands"), Mark Lockwood, Kevin Zimmer, James Paton, and a wide variety of tour guides and casual observers. A special contribution came from David Sibley, who unexpectedly found a Black-capped Chickadee specimen from the Trans-Pecos at Yale's Peabody Museum. It is currently the only known specimen from Texas. Finally, the Dallas Museum of Natural History played a very special role in allowing us the luxury of time and access to a wide variety of records and study skins.

We would like to give a special thanks to our wives, Gretchen and Yvonne. As the writing progressed, they made a courteous and unexpected leap from birding widows to computer widows. As always, we are in their debt.

ABOUT THE BOOK

Birds of the Trans-Pecos will be an important companion guide for those interested in the bird life of the Trans-Pecos, Texas. The book is best used as a database of bird species found in the Trans-Pecos and their preferred habitats. Unlike other published material on the area's avifauna, it covers the entire Trans-Pecos geographic region (defined below) and all of Val Verde County.

It is a fact that few people come to the Trans-Pecos to visit any single destination. Travelers generally come by car and drive to several different locations within the area. Most often visited are national parks, state parks, historical sites, and recreational lakes. Published information on the bird life at these locations may be accurate, but details are frequently outdated and the big picture may be missing altogether.

The authors' intent in writing *Birds of the Trans-Pecos* is to put together, in a useful format, the scattered and puzzling pieces of information that make up the area's ornithological sightings. Clearly, only the foundation is being laid. Much more work is needed, particularly in the mountain ranges where reports are rare and very irregular.

Birds of the Trans-Pecos is not meant to be used as a quick reference guide to birding hot spots, a life histories book of selected species, or an illustrated field guide. It is a simple annotated list of birds. It represents several years of research and concerns a unique and remote area in the southwestern United States.

The Trans-Pecos area outlined in this book is a place where unique ecological zones meet. East meets west (areas where Acadian Flycatchers nest near Gray Vireos), and north meets south (areas where Red Crossbills nest near Common Black-Hawks). Added to this ecological stew is the close proximity of the Mexican deserts, the Mexican mountains, the Colorado Plateau, the great U.S. prairies, the south Texas brushland, and the Edwards Plateau. All of these ecological areas are represented in the Trans-Pecos.

Birds of the Trans-Pecos is driven from the perspective that birds show a certain fidelity for specific habitats. In the Trans-Pecos, the various microhabitats and the associated bird species bear this out. Birds choose where to live and generally are loyal, year after year, to those areas where they experience the most success.

As an example of such site fidelity, an entire population (well over thirty-five pairs) of Gray Flycatchers was recently discovered nesting in a small pocket of habitat on the north slope of one Trans-Pecos mountain. Not one other nesting pair has been found within the state of Texas. For many birds like the Gray Flycatcher, a small creek on the north slope of a mountain would be considered acceptable habitat while the rest of the Trans-Pecos would not. If this book contains any moral message, it is to point out the importance of protecting these small, but unique, habitats.

Because the human population is so small in the Trans-Pecos, the historical database of bird observations is limited. Yet much has been accomplished with a few avid observers. Observers who have added critical information to this book include ranchers, tourists, bird-watchers, researchers, park rangers, and tour guides. Some were looking for a highly sought-after bird rarity. Others were just born curious and had the good sense to report their findings. Much work is still needed.

Only two other books are available at this time with information specific to the bird life of this area. Roland H. Wauer's book entitled *A Field Guide to the Birds of the Big Bend* is recommended for those traveling to Big Bend National Park to see birds. Edward Kutac's *Birder's Guide to Texas* is a site guide to birding spots in Texas and has some particularly relevant information on the location of Trans-Pecos birds. Another book by R. H. Wauer, entitled *Birding*

Texas (1998), may also add information on birding locations in the Trans-Pecos. For visual identification, the National Geographic Society's *Field Guide to the Birds of North America* and the Peterson Field Guide series of *Western Birds* by Roger Tory Peterson remain the most commonly used illustrated field guides for Trans-Pecos bird-watching.

THE TRANS-PECOS

THE AREA in Texas defined as the Trans-Pecos (Trans-Pecos means "across the Pecos River") is an area in western Texas perhaps better known for its human history than its natural history. It is likely that more people have heard of Judge Roy Bean than have heard of the Chihuahuan Desert. Yet this area west of the Pecos is nearly the size of West Virginia and has a wider variety of recorded bird life than the state of New York.

By definition, the Trans-Pecos area in this book will refer to the entire Texas area west of the Pecos River which runs from northwest of Pecos, Texas (Loving County), to the southeast near the city of Del Rio, Texas (Val Verde County). Because of the extensive public access around Lake Amistad near Del Rio, this book includes all of Val Verde County. All other counties, however, follow the "west-of-the-Pecos-River" rule in regard to the recorded bird life.

Also, by definition, the Trans-Pecos area is almost entirely within the Chihuahuan Desert biotic province—a desert ecosystem that can be defined by several indicator plants. Two places mentioned in this book are not entirely part of the Chihuahuan Desert biotic province. The Lake Amistad area near Del Rio, Texas, and the Guadalupe Mountains near the border of New Mexico both have partial relationships to other adjoining ecosystems. The nature of the Chihuahuan Desert biotic province is outlined below.

The use of the term "Big Bend country" in the species accounts and other parts of the book refers to the southern three-fourths of Brewster and Presidio counties. This area is a unique desert environment with specialized plant and animal communities.

THE GEOGRAPHY

The Trans-Pecos landscape contains several habitats and microhabitats. These habitats range from desert shrub to pine forests, with an elevational range from 1,800 ft. to over 8,750 ft. Rainfall is seasonal, with most of it falling in late summer. Rivers and creeks are generally scarce at all elevations, with most of the water located within the Rio Grande and Pecos River watersheds.

As a broad rule, the lowest and driest areas in the Trans-Pecos are referred to as *shrub desert*. This desert yields to what is known as a *desert grassland* on some mountain slopes and at higher elevations. At still higher elevations, the desert grasslands change to what is known as *plains grasslands*—distinguished by a somewhat different plant community. This grassland begins to yield to a grassy oak-juniper woodland at approximately 5,000 ft. and finally to a largely coniferous woodland at higher elevations. On high, rocky wind-blown peaks, the vegetation is stunted or absent altogether.

Riparian vegetation along the Rio Grande and other rivers and streams offers yet another type of habitat for the area's wildlife. Here, galleries of cottonwood trees and a sometimes thick shrub component offer food and cover for a variety of birds.

The avifauna and the ecological zones within the Trans-Pecos are closely related. Birds seem to prefer habitat "types" for various occupations. For some birds, a single habitat is all that's required. For others, the various occupations may include one habitat type for nesting and another for feeding. More commonly, the habitat being sought may change with the season—a different ecological requirement in summer from the one chosen in winter. Although birding by habitat type is generally a good idea, it is an oversimplification to assume a bird's presence based solely on geography.

The information presented here on vegetation and habitat is quite general in nature and based solely on what is seen by the visitor on a typical visit. For a more thorough look at the Trans-Pecos vegetation, one may wish to pick up A. M. Powell's *Trees and Shrubs of Trans-Pecos Texas* (1988).

THE DESERT

Vast expanses of Chihuahuan Desert cover the Trans-Pecos region. This desert is at a relatively high elevation, with a general range of between 1,800 and 5,000 ft. The true look of the Chihuahuan Desert is a climatic equation that relies on a combination of elevation, soil type, rainfall, and angle of the sun.

The Chihuahuan Desert is generally characterized by cool winters with regular and somewhat numerous freezes and low annual rainfall ranging from 7.5 to 12 in. Precipitation falls mostly in late summer and early fall, though there are some winter rains and occasional snows as well.

These climatic factors combined with typically high calcium soils produce a distinctive plant community. Creosote Bush (*Larrea tridentata*) and Tarbush (*Flourensia cernua*) are excellent indicators of true Chihuahuan Desert. Other typical species include Lechuguilla (*Agave lechuguilla*), Honey Mesquite (*Prosopis glandulosa*), Snakeweed (*Xanthocephalum sphaerocephalum*), Soaptree Yucca (*Yucca elata*), Four-wing Saltbush (*Atriplex canescens*), and various cacti species (with Prickly Pears and Chollas being most conspicuous). Desert washes are often lined with Little Leaf Sumac (*Rhus microphylla*), Apache Plume (*Fallugia paradoxa*), and Desert Willow (*Chilopsis linearis*). Common roadside plants include Buffalo Gourd (*Cucurbita foetidissima*) and the non-native Russian Thistle (*Salsola kali*) or "tumbleweed."

In higher areas where desert and grassland meet (with the distinction between the two being difficult to draw), there are more yuccas as well as Sotol (*Dasylirion leiophyllum*) and Sacahuista (*Nolina texana*). The desert is often carpeted with wildflowers, especially in spring and late summer, and includes the likes of Desert Marigold (*Baileya multiradiata*), Desert Zinnia (*Zinnia grandiflora*), and Desert Verbena (*Verbena wrightii*), to name but a few. Other desert color is provided by the brilliant red blossoms of the Ocotillo (*Fouquieria splendens*), the showy white stalks of the Soaptree Yucca, and the gorgeous lavender flowers of Cenizo (*Leucophyllum frutescens, L. candidum*, and *L. minus*). Cenizo is known sometimes as Barometer Bush for its tendency to bloom overnight after a rain.

Although birds like the Black-throated Sparrow frequent this desert shrub habitat, it is generally the habitat with the fewest number of bird species.

THE GRASSLANDS

Grasslands are one of the most widespread vegetation communities in North America and are an important ecosystem in the Trans-Pecos. Although grassland communities within the Chihuahuan Desert region of the Trans-Pecos are remarkably diverse, casual visitors will recognize only one fairly homogeneous and fairly widespread grassland type.

These grasslands reach about 2 ft. in height and represent one of the largest contiguous areas of grassland vegetation in the southwestern United States. This habitat type can best be experienced in the Marathon-Alpine-Marfa-Valentine corridor along U.S Highway 90. In general, grasslands of the Trans-Pecos occupy gently rolling terrain of intermountain basins and lower slopes and plateaus at mid-elevations up to about 5,200 ft. They are apparent on the flanks of the Davis Mountains but also are represented at mid-elevations in the Chisos Mountains, as well as lapping up onto the lower eastern slopes of the Chinati and the Sierra Vieja mountains. An extensive area of grassland also occurs on the Diablo Platform, the plateau bounded on the east by the Sierra Diablo and on the west by the Hueco mountains.

Grasslands are maintained in large measure by rainfall and soil conditions, but natural wildfires also have played an important role. Fires, occurring primarily in spring and early summer, are initiated by the usually dry lightning storms during this season. At this time, the grasses are normally still dormant, awaiting the monsoonal summer rains that begin in July and last through September or until frost in the fall.

These grass-dominated communities, known as *pastizal* in Spanish, are usually called semidesert grassland or, by some, desert plains grasslands. Because they occur at mid-elevations and usually have greater than 10 in. of annual rainfall, *semidesert grassland* is probably the more ecologically correct term. These grassy communities bound the Chihuahuan Desert on the north and east and separate the Chihuahuan from the Sonoran desert on the west. They are dominated by Blue Grama (*Bouteloua* sp.), with interspersed yucca, beargrass, sotol, or agaves. These grasslands are home to large herds of pronghorns and large numbers of rodents. As a consequence, this habitat attracts numerous wintering raptors and formerly supported Aplomado Falcons. The Trans-Pecos grasslands also support an amazing array of wintering sparrows, particularly during winters after wet autumns. Thirteen grassland sparrows have been found in these extensive grasslands.

Within the Trans-Pecos, such temperate grasslands are at the northeastern extreme of their distribution. Above these grasslands, and often interfingering all along their upper environmental limit, are evergreen, oak, juniper, and pinyon woodlands.

For further reading, see A. Michael Powell, *Grasses of the Trans-Pecos and Adjacent Areas* (1994).

THE MOUNTAINS

Three major mountain ranges dot the Texas Trans-Pecos landscape from northwest to southeast. The Guadalupe Mountains on the New Mexico border are largely sedimentary rock and have the highest Texas mountain peak in El Capitan at 8,750 ft. The Davis Mountains are in the center of the Trans-Pecos. They are volcanic in origin and have more surface area above 5,000 ft. than the other two mountain ranges. The Chisos Mountains, located within Big Bend National Park, are also volcanic and contain some of the most rugged and beautiful scenery found anywhere in the United States.

Just 40 miles below the U.S. border in northern Coahuila, Mexico, and within visual proximity to Big Bend National Park are the Sierra Del Carmen Mountains. This mountain range is worth mentioning here because of its montane forests and specialized avifauna. These mountains are greater in mass and elevation than any of the mountains within the Trans-Pecos. Much of the mountain range seen from the U.S. side of the Rio Grande is largely limestone, but the very highest parts of the Sierra Del Carmen range are volcanic in origin (and are occasionally referred to separately as the Maderas Del Carmen Mountains). The vegetation and avifauna in these mountains are perhaps more reminiscent of the montane vegetation in southeast Arizona than of any place in Texas. In the high forests of the Sierra Del Carmen range, large stands of Southwestern white pines harbor nesting birds like the Olive Warbler and Yellow-eyed Junco which are accidental in Texas.

These four major mountain ranges (and many of the minor ones) resemble a kind of stepping-stone island chain. Their remote nature makes for a very exclusive bird habitat within a large geographical radius. They are wooded islands in a sea of desert. Over time, the bird life in these mountains has become so acclimated to specific environments that many species rarely stray from their home territory. Both of the aforementioned bird species, the Olive Warbler and Yellow-eyed Junco, currently have a combined total of only eight documented sightings in Texas even though they nest less than 50 miles south of the Rio Grande!

These four mountain ranges differ in habitat and vegetation just enough to vary the distribution of several bird species. Virginia's Warbler, for example, will nest in the Guadalupe and Davis mountains, but not in the Chisos or Sierra Del Carmen. For the closely related Colima Warbler, however, the exact opposite is true. Interestingly, there are several species that have selected only a single mountain range within the Texas border as a preferred nesting habitat. These birds nest in other states, and, at first glance, appear to have appropriate nesting options in several mountainous areas in the Trans-Pecos. Yet, for whatever reason, these birds have chosen not to nest beyond their one definitive single mountain range in the state of Texas. These species include the Gray Flycatcher, Mexican Jay, Juniper Titmouse, Colima Warbler, Dark-eyed (Gray-headed) Junco, and possibly one or two other species whose status is still uncertain. This exclusive site-fidelity reinforces the notion that the Trans-Pecos mountains are an oasis for many birds, and that this montane habitat is critical to the success of several Trans-Pecos species.

Although not on the scale of the four major mountain ranges, other mountain ranges like the Chinati and Franklin mountains play an important role in regards to local weather and the movements of birds. These smaller ranges are not known to harbor any unusual or exclusive bird species. However, it should be pointed out that many of these smaller ranges have limited public access, and future research may yield new discoveries.

THE NESTING BIRDS
OF THE TRANS-PECOS MOUNTAINS

Table 1 is a comparative list of the nesting species within the Guadalupe, Davis, and Chisos mountain ranges in the U.S., and the Sierra Del Carmen Mountains of northern Mexico. The original research for this chart was completed by Wauer and Ligon and taken from the *Transactions of the Symposium on the Biological Resources of the Chihuahuan Desert Region, United States and Mexico,* edited by Wauer and Riskind (1974), and updated by Bryan and Zimmer in 1994 and Peterson and Zimmer in 1997. The authors of *Birds of the Trans-Pecos* have taken the liberty of changing certain bird names from the 1974 list to coincide with the newer name changes as supplemented by the American Ornithologists' Union (a.o.u.).

Species in this list exhibit regular or occasional nesting in areas at or above 5,000 ft., as reflected in the key below. Significant discoveries have occurred since the information was published in 1974. An asterisk (*) indicates a status change or, in a few cases, a species addition to the 1974 list.

X	Regular Nester	?	Possible Nester
R	Rare or Local Nester	H	Historical Nester
P	Probable Nester		

TABLE 1

THE NESTING BIRDS OF THE TRANS-PECOS MOUNTAINS

NESTING BIRDS	GUAD.	DAVIS	CHISOS	CARMEN
Turkey Vulture	X	X	X	X
Sharp-shinned Hawk *	X	?	?	X
Cooper's Hawk	X	X		X
Northern Goshawk				?
Common Black-Hawk *		X		
Zone-Tailed Hawk	P	X	X	X
Red-Tailed Hawk	X	X	X	X
Golden Eagle	X	X	X	X
American Kestrel	X	X	X	X
Prairie Falcon	X	X	X	
Peregrine Falcon *	X	H	X	X

NESTING BIRDS	GUAD.	DAVIS	CHISOS	CARMEN
Wild Turkey *	X	X	?	X
Montezuma Quail *	H	X	H	X
Band-tailed Pigeon	X	X	X	X
White-winged Dove *	P	X	X	X
Mourning Dove	X	X	X	X
Greater Roadrunner *		P		
Flammulated Owl *	X	X	R	X
Western Screech-Owl	X	X	X	X
Great Horned Owl	X	X	X	X
Northern Pygmy Owl *		?		X
Elf Owl *	R	R	?	X
Spotted Owl *	X	R		
Northern Saw-Whet Owl *	X	P		X
Common Nighthawk	X	X		X
Common Poorwill	X	X	X	X
Whip-poor-will	X	X	X	X
White-throated Swift	X	X	X	X
White-eared Hummingbird *		?		
Blue-throated Hummingbird *	R		X	X
Magnificent Hummingbird *	X	X	X	X
Lucifer Hummingbird			X	X
Black-chinned Hummingbird	X	X	X	X
Broad-tailed Hummingbird	X	X	X	X
Acorn Woodpecker	X	X	X	X
Ladder-backed Woodpecker	X	X	X	X
Hairy Woodpecker	X			P
Northern Flicker	X	X	X	X
Olive-sided Flycatcher *	X	P		

NESTING BIRDS	GUAD.	DAVIS	CHISOS	CARMEN
Western Wood-Pewee	X	X		?
Dusky Flycatcher *	?			
Gray Flycatcher *	?	X		
Cordilleran Flycatcher	X	X	X	X
Black Phoebe *	X	X	X	X
Say's Phoebe	X	X	X	X
Dusky-capped Flycatcher *		P		
Ash-throated Flycatcher	X	X	X	X
Cassin's Kingbird	X	X		
Loggerhead Shrike *	?	X	?	?
Black-capped Vireo			X	X
Gray Vireo *	X	R	X	X
Plumbeous Vireo *	X	X	R	X
Hutton's Vireo	X	X	X	X
Warbling Vireo	X	X	?	
Steller's Jay	X	X		
Western Scrub-Jay *	X	X	X	
Mexican Jay			X	X
Common Raven	X	X	X	X
Violet-green Swallow	X	X	X	X
Barn Swallow *	?	X	X	
Mountain Chickadee	X	X		
Juniper Titmouse	X			
Tufted "Black-crested" Titmouse		X	X	X
Bushtit	X	X	X	X
Red-breasted Nuthatch *	R			
White-breasted Nuthatch	X	X	X	X
Pygmy Nuthatch	X	X		X

NESTING BIRDS	GUAD.	DAVIS	CHISOS	CARMEN
Brown Creeper *	X	?		
Cactus Wren	X	X	X	X
Rock Wren	X	X	X	X
Canyon Wren	X	X	X	X
Bewick's Wren	X	X	X	X
House Wren *	X	X		X
Blue-gray Gnatcatcher *	X	R	X	X
Western Bluebird	X	X		X
Hermit Thrush	X	X		
American Robin *	X	X		
Northern Mockingbird	X	X	X	X
Curve-billed Thrasher	X	X	X	X
Crissal Thrasher *		R	X	X
Phainopepla *		X	R	
Olive Warbler				X
Orange-crowned Warbler *	X	X		
Virginia's Warbler *	X	X		
Colima Warbler			X	X
Yellow-rumped Warbler *	X	X		
Black-throated Gray Warbler *	H			
Grace's Warbler	X	X		
MacGillivray's Warbler *		?		
Painted Redstart *		R	R	X
Hepatic Tanager	X	X	X	X
Summer Tanager	X	X	X	X
Western Tanager *	X	X	?	
Green-tailed Towhee *	X	X	?	?
Spotted Towhee	X	X	X	X

NESTING BIRDS	GUAD.	DAVIS	CHISOS	CARMEN
Canyon Towhee	X	X	X	X
Rufous-crowned Sparrow	X	X	X	X
Chipping Sparrow	X	X		
Black-chinned Sparrow	X	X	X	X
Lark Sparrow *		X		?
"Gray-headed" Junco	X			
Yellow-eyed Junco				X
Black-headed Grosbeak	X	X	X	X
Blue Grosbeak	X	X	X	X
Eastern Meadowlark *		X	?	
Brewer's Blackbird *		H		
Bronzed Cowbird *		X	?	?
Brown-headed Cowbird	X	X	X	X
Scott's Oriole	X	X	X	X
House Finch	X	X	X	X
Red Crossbill *	X	R		?
Pine Siskin	X	R		P
Lesser Goldfinch	X	X	X	X
Regular Nester (X)	81	80	59	72
Rare/Local Nester (R)	3	8	4	0
Probable Nester (P)	2	5	0	2
Possible Nester (?)	4	5	9	7
Historical Nester (Prior to 1974)	2	2	1	0
Known/Potential Breeders	92	100	73	81

THE PARKS, RESERVOIRS,
AND RECREATIONAL LAKES

Several species of birds have found safe haven in the large park systems that are found in the Trans-Pecos. In the entire United States, for example, the Colima Warbler nests only in the high elevations of Big Bend National Park. These state and national parks provide some natural continuity of habitat that would be difficult to maintain without government protection. Certain ranchers have also provided some ecological stability, and their property has proven to be equally important—particularly in the Davis Mountains. It is the parks, however, which have the most concentrated areas of undisturbed natural habitat. This special habitat is critical for the survival of the Trans-Pecos wildlife.

Some of the parks, reservoirs, and recreational lakes found in the Trans-Pecos are so special in regard to their bird life that they warrant a broader discussion. These areas generally have some unique natural quality and frequently contain the widest variety of bird life. However, the list that follows does not necessarily represent the best bird-watching areas in the Trans-Pecos. Each area mentioned here is listed because of its unique habitat that, in turn, has invited a unique variety of bird species.

For information on special access, checklists, or entrance fees, individuals should contact each park separately.

Amistad National Recreation Area
and Seminole Canyon State Park (Val Verde County)
Phone: 915/292-4464
Acreage: 2,172
Checklist: Weidenfeld 1989
Key Species: White-throated Swift

This large lake and park system is on the eastern edge of the Trans-Pecos. All of this lake is actually just east of the Pecos River, but is included here because of the habitat similarities to the Trans-Pecos and the large public access areas. The entire area is actually in a confluence of the Trans-Pecos, Edwards Plateau, and South Texas Brushland ecological zones.

Lake Amistad is a large recreational lake not particularly well known for its birds. It does, however, contain birds such as the

Black-bellied Whistling-Duck, Green Kingfisher, and Great Kiskadee that are at the limit of their range from adjoining areas. On the lake, many ducks, cormorants, and herons can be found during certain seasons. Around the perimeter of the lake is one of the better places to look for the Golden-fronted Woodpecker and an occasional Harris' Hawk.

Balmorhea State Park (Reeves County)
Phone: 915/375-2370
Acreage: 45
Checklist: Lockwood 1992
Key Species: Migrants, Marsh Species

Balmorhea State Park is located near the town of Balmorhea just north of the Davis Mountains. This small state park has a unique spring that is routed through the park, making it good for birdwatching during most seasons. The park is very good for sparrows in the winter months. Painted Buntings and Lesser Goldfinches are seen regularly in the summer.

Big Bend National Park/Chisos Mountains (Brewster County)
Phone: 915/477-2251
Acreage: 801,000 .
Checklist: Park Service 1994
Key Species: Colima Warbler, Lucifer Hummingbird

This park has recorded more bird species (at least 460) than any other national park in the country. It has the only recorded nesting Colima Warblers found in the United States. A few species that are not found in other parts of Texas can, with some effort, be found here.

In summer, the lower elevations support Lucifer Hummingbirds, Elf Owls, Lucy's Warblers, and Hooded Orioles. The Chisos Mountains harbor Band-tailed Pigeons, Mexican Jays, and Hepatic Tanagers. Varied Buntings are found in several areas. Gray and Black-capped vireos are uncommon but are seen with some regularity in spring and summer. Along the Rio Grande floodplain, irregular species like Thick-billed Kingbirds have nested in years past. Even some eastern migrants, such as the Black-throated Blue Warbler, have found their way to this remote area. Because of the proximity to Mexico, a North American rarity like the Tufted Flycatcher will occasionally pay a visit to the park.

There are several options for the bird-watcher at any time of year, but spring is undoubtedly the best window of time for birding in Big Bend. On a good spring weekend, the birding may be hot and exhausting, but it nearly always is rewarding.

Big Bend Ranch State Park (Presidio County)
Phone: 915/229-3416
Acreage: 268,495
Checklist: In Progress
Key Species: Riparian Species, Desert Shrub Species

The Big Bend Ranch State Park (referred to here as Big Bend Ranch) is a relatively recent acquisition of desert property by the Texas Parks and Wildlife Department. This area is so large that its acquisition nearly doubled the size of state-owned park property in Texas. Big Bend Ranch is only about an hour west of Big Bend National Park. It is dominated by Chihuahuan Desert grasslands over at least 75% of its acreage. Here, the canyons and arroyos support rich thickets of desert thornscrub. The scores of springs scattered over the Big Bend Ranch landscape support very local cottonwood gallery woodlands where the bird life is correspondingly rich. Migrants such as Townsend's Warbler and Western Tanager are seen with some frequency in this cottonwood grove habitat.

The birds along the Rio Grande corridor are especially diverse during migration as birds naturally funnel through here. Except during unusual weather circumstances, the Big Bend Ranch is nearly devoid of any montane avifauna. It is, however, one of the premier spots for observation of typical northern Chihuahuan Desert birds. Although not abundant, Varied Bunting is perhaps more common throughout this park than in other areas of the Trans-Pecos.

At present, access to Big Bend Ranch is by permit only. The 35-mile interior gravel road is well maintained, and there are several miles of 4-wheel drive trails. (Scenic FM 170 follows the Rio Grande along the southern edge of the park.) A bus tour of the area can be arranged, but access to good birding spots would be somewhat limited under this condition. Contact the park for more details about special access or bus tours.

Chinati Mountains State Park (Presidio County)
Phone: None (Currently Not Open to Public)
Acreage: 40,000
Checklist: None
Key Species: Montane Species, Grassland Species

Located in western Presidio County. At this writing, the park is not open, and there is little information on its avifauna. This mountain area, however, has a broad range of elevation and may prove to be good habitat for a wide variety of birds.

Davis Mountains and Davis Mountains State Park
(Jeff Davis County)
Phone: 915/426-3337
Acreage: 2,677
Checklist: In Progress
Key Species: Montezuma Quail, Phainopepla

The state park, the town of Fort Davis, and the Davis Mountains as a whole all lie within Jeff Davis County. The state park lies just north of the town of Fort Davis. Centrally located in the Trans-Pecos, this entire park is at an elevation that makes it unique within the Chihuahuan Desert ecosystem. Both the park and the town of Fort Davis lie at about a 5,000-ft. elevation. The state park itself is largely a high-elevation grassland habitat with scattered oaks and junipers.

This park is the prime spot for viewing Montezuma Quail in the Trans-Pecos (and perhaps the U.S.). At certain seasons, there is a feeding station where the birds come to feed in morning and evening. This station is occasionally staffed by volunteers and usually offers very good looks at this hard-to-see species. Other birds that frequent the park include Phainopepla, Black-headed Grosbeak, and Cassin's Kingbird in summer, as well as permanent residents such as Acorn Woodpecker and Western Scrub-Jay throughout the year. If one is lucky, the uncommon Black-chinned Sparrow can occasionally be found within the park boundary. In breeding season, Common Black-Hawks have nested in cottonwood trees just outside the park along Limpia Creek.

Beginning at about 6,000 ft. on the north side of the Davis

Mountains and outside the state park is an evergreen forest ecosystem that includes Ponderosa Pine, Mexican Pinyon Pine, and, in the higher elevations, Limber Pine. This remnant coniferous forest is home to several bird species unique within the Trans-Pecos. The coniferous forest habitat in this mountain range, however, is largely on private property and has no public access. Several property owners have been helpful in recent research efforts, but a thorough understanding of the high-elevation Davis Mountains avifauna is not yet available. New ornithological discoveries will likely continue to come from that area.

Devils River State Natural Area (Val Verde County)
Phone: 210/395-2133
Acreage: 19,988
Checklist: In Progress
Key Species: Black-capped Vireo, Gray Vireo

Devils River is located north of the city of Del Rio. It is at the confluence of the Tamaulipan, Balconian, and Chihuahuan biotic regions of Texas. Because of the habitat diversity, there is a corresponding richness of flora and fauna. Habitat varies from riparian woodlands of oak and pecan to intermittent drainages with sycamore galleries. Drier slopes support semidesert grasslands and, where conditions are more severe, a xeric (dry) scrub. The mesa tops are a mosaic of grassland and shrubland habitats. There are isolated pinyon woodlands in the area, and occasionally Ashe Juniper can be found on favorable canyon slopes. The best areas for birding are along the permanent watercourses, especially where there remain gallery woodlands.

This area is known for species that most regularly occur east of the Trans-Pecos. Riparian areas in spring and summer have been known to harbor Acadian Flycatchers and Eastern Wood-Pewees. Drier areas are habitat for nesting Black-capped Vireos.

Franklin Mountains State Park (El Paso County)
Phone: 915/566-6441
Acreage: 23,810
Checklist: Zimmer 1996
Key Species: Gambel's Quail, Crissal Thrasher

The Franklin Mountains State Park begins near downtown El Paso and runs northward to the Texas–New Mexico border. The eastern face of the mountain range supports more vegetation than the drier, more exposed western face. The diversity of birds is correspondingly greater on the eastern slope.

Vegetation within the state park is typical of the Chihuahuan Desert, with plant communities dominated by Creosote Bush, Lechuguilla, and Four-wing Saltbush. In the high elevations, there are stands of oaks, hackberries, and ash. The few springs found at the higher locations act as magnets to resident and migrating birds. Resident species include Golden Eagle, Scaled Quail, White-throated Swift, Verdin, Canyon Wren, Black-throated Sparrow, and Pyrrhuloxia. Migration (April–May and August–October) may bring a variety of western migrants, such as Hammond's and Dusky flycatchers and Townsend's, Hermit, and Black-throated Gray warblers.

Guadalupe Mountains and Guadalupe Mountains National Park
(Culberson and Hudspeth Counties)
Phone: 915/828-3251
Acreage: 86,416
Checklist: Park Service 1997
Key Species: Juniper Titmouse, Virginia's Warbler

The Guadalupe Mountains National Park is on the northern edge of the Texas Trans-Pecos. Most access to the park is from the Culberson County side. In terms of its flora, this park may only partially fit into the Trans-Pecos Chihuahuan Desert ecosystem. The higher elevations of this park are at times more reminiscent of the southern Rocky Mountains or the Colorado Plateau than the Chihuahuan Desert. Because they share features with both of these ecosystems, the Guadalupe Mountains harbor an interesting variety of bird life.

This park appears to have the only stable population of Juniper Titmouse in the state of Texas. It is also the best place to look for Grace's and Virginia's warblers, which nest in the higher canyons. In the very highest areas of pine forests (access is by hiking only) Flammulated Owl, Cordilleran Flycatcher, Pygmy Nuthatch, Western Tanager, and Red Crossbill all appear to be fairly common during the summer months. In contrast, the lowest elevations have produced winter records of Sage Sparrow and other desert species.

Juniper Titmouse

Vagrant species could also show up in this park given its location. Rocky Mountain birds like Clark's Nutcracker and American Dipper, which are considered Texas rarities, would more than likely make a Trans-Pecos appearance in the Guadalupe Mountains. Unusual Texas residents like the Spotted Owl have also been recorded from this mountain range.

Hueco Tanks State Historical Park (El Paso County)
Phone: 915/857-1135
Acreage: 860
Checklist: Zimmer 1996
Key Species: Crissal Thrasher, White-throated Swift

This park is only a half-hour east of El Paso, Texas. It lies in a dry desert shrub environment dominated by Creosote Bush. It is unique, however, in having a large outcrop of granitic rock with numerous small canyons and washes. Indian petroglyphs are found around the caves and crevices of this outcrop. There is usually some water at all seasons, which makes it attractive to birds.

Hueco Tanks may be the most accessible place to look for White-throated Swift or Crissal Thrasher in Texas at any time of year. In migration, birds like the Dusky or Hammond's flycatcher can be fairly common on one day, while the next day's star attraction may be MacGillivray's Warbler. Scaled Quail and Golden Eagle are frequent park visitors. If one is fortunate, Prairie Falcon may be seen. Winter generally brings good concentrations of sparrows, including Brewer's and occasionally Black-chinned. In some years, Eastern, Western, and Mountain bluebirds are all possible.

Lake Balmorhea (Reeves County)
(Not State-owned Property)

Lake Balmorhea is located just south of the town of Balmorhea. It should not be confused with Balmorhea State Park, which is a few miles west of the lake. This recreational lake is a prime fishing location for many Texans. There is a general store near the dam where one must pay a small fee to bird-watch. Generally, this lake has been very good for bird-watching in winter, spring, and fall and has produced an inordinate number of bird rarities for Texas. On November 27, 1993, Red-throated Loon, Yellow-billed Loon, and Snow Bunting all made an appearance around the lake on the same day! Western Grebe and Clark's Grebe (and even some hybrids) can often be seen regularly from certain vantage points around the lake. Songbirds in the area can range from Sedge Wren to Pyrrhuloxia.

LESSER-KNOWN BIRDING AREAS

The following list of lesser-known birding sites is not comprehensive but represents several unique areas that harbor a wide variety of birds. It should be noted, however, that state natural areas, wildlife management areas, and Texas Nature Conservancy property generally require special permission before one can enter. Individuals should contact the appropriate agencies before the date of their arrival.

Furthermore, many reservoirs and parks have limited public access, and most should be considered "remote" destinations. *It is important for anyone traveling in the Trans-Pecos to have a clear understanding of property rights and road conditions before traveling in remote areas.*

Black Gap Wildlife Management Area (Brewster County)

Located near the eastern entrance of Big Bend National Park and known for a wide variety of desert birds.

Chandler Independence Creek Preserve (Terrell County)

A Texas Nature Conservancy area located 22 miles south of Sheffield in northern Terrell County. The habitat here is a unique riparian habitat bordered by oaks, willows, mesquite, and junipers. Several species of vireos and other songbirds can be found on the property. Visitors must have permission from the Texas Nature Conservancy.

Fort Bliss Sewage Ponds (El Paso County)

Located northeast of the city of El Paso. Known for waterfowl, wading birds, and shorebirds, as well as migrant passerines. An astounding 302 species have been documented at this one location. Unusual records included Glossy Ibis, Eurasian Wigeon, White-winged and Surf scoters, Masked Duck, Red-necked Stint, Ruff, Red Phalarope, Western and Sabine's gulls, and Lawrence's Goldfinch. Gambel's Quail and Crissal Thrasher are regular breeders.

Fort Hancock Reservoir (Hudspeth County)

Located in southern Hudspeth County near the Rio Grande. Known for waterfowl, wading birds, and gulls. Nesting Neotropical Cormorants occur in spring and summer. Unusual site records include Brown Pelican, Tricolored Heron, Eurasian Wigeon, Black Scoter, and Mew and Thayer's gulls.

Imperial Reservoir (Pecos County)

Located on the northern edge of Pecos County. Known for waterfowl and wading birds. Unusual records have included Pacific Loon,

Roseate Spoonbill, Black-legged Kittiwake, and nesting Snowy Plovers.

McNary Reservoir (Hudspeth County)

Located in southern Hudspeth County near the Rio Grande. Known for waterfowl, wading birds, and gulls. Both Western and Clark's grebes are present in numbers most winters, and occasionally in the summer as well. Unusual records include Pacific Loon, Eurasian Wigeon, Long-tailed Jaeger, Sabine's and California gulls, and nesting Neotropic Cormorants and Great Egrets.

Red Bluff Reservoir (Reeves and Loving Counties)

This lake is divided equally between both counties. Known for waterfowl and wading birds. Unusual records include Pacific Loon, Roseate Spoonbill, Parasitic Jaeger, and Black-legged Kittiwake.

Tornillo Reservoir (El Paso County)

Located in southeastern El Paso County near the Rio Grande. Known for waterfowl. Brown Pelican, Eurasian Wigeon, and Barrow's Goldeneye have been recorded at this reservoir.

Toyah Lake (Reeves County)

Located southeast of the city of Pecos. Known for waterfowl, wading birds, and shorebirds. Nesting Snowy Plovers have been observed on this lake.

Most of the state parks have bird checklists that can be acquired from Texas Parks and Wildlife. Maps and more specific information about the best bird-watching areas in the Trans-Pecos can be found in Ed Kutac's *Birding in Texas*.

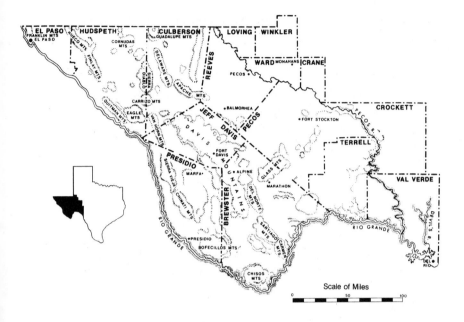

Map 1. *Trans-Pecos Region of Texas and adjacent counties with major geographical features and towns (from Powell 1988, used with permission)*

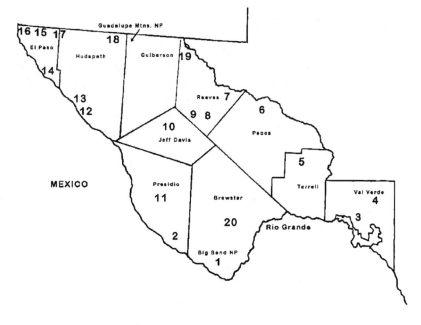

Map 2. *Selected areas for Trans-Pecos bird-watching that are outlined in this book*

1. Big Bend National Park
2. Big Bend Ranch State Park
3. Lake Amistad and Seminole Canyon State Park
4. Devils River State Natural Area
5. Chandler Independence Creek Preserve
6. Imperial Reservoir
7. Lake Toyah
8. Lake Balmorhea
9. Balmorhea State Park
10. Davis Mountains State Park
11. Chinati Mountains State Park
12. McNary Reservoir
13. Fort Hancock Reservoir
14. Tornillo Reservoir
15. Fort Bliss Sewage Ponds
16. Franklin Mountains State Park
17. Hueco Tanks State Park
18. Guadalupe Mountains National Park
19. Red Bluff Reservoir
20. Black Gap Wildlife Management Area

THE HUMAN ELEMENT

Because of the small number of people living there, the Trans-Pecos remains relatively undisturbed. The human population within this largely desert environment is so minuscule that there are counties the size of Rhode Island with less than 2,000 people. The topography in this rugged country can be unforgiving and does not invite many farmers or casual homesteaders (although ranching is done successfully in some areas). Water is such a valuable commodity that most outdoor occupations require resourcefulness and intelligent planning. Historically, many people have ventured to the Trans-Pecos to try and make a living off the land, but only the hardiest of souls have succeeded.

Most people living in the Trans-Pecos confine themselves to the large metropolis of El Paso (population about 530,797) or small urban centers where industry and business can thrive (Del Rio, Pecos, and Fort Stockton, Texas). Most other areas can only be described as rural.

As everywhere, there have been significant changes in the Trans-Pecos landscape. Certain mining ventures and the overgrazing of domestic animals historically have had an impact on the ecology of the Chihuahuan Desert. The control of natural fires also has played a role in shaping the overall plant community in this ecosystem, particularly at higher elevations. The use of water resources and the building of large power plants may have some future effect on this fragile desert environment. In a relative sense, however, even with many changes in its human and geological history, the Trans-Pecos still looks much the same as it did five hundred years ago.

THE TRANS-PECOS BIRDS

THE DIVERSITY of the avifauna in the Trans-Pecos can be attrib-
uted to the wide variety of habitat types. A two-hour drive from
Marathon, Texas, to the McDonald Observatory near Fort Davis is a
drive from desert shrub to an evergreen forest and illustrates the
incredible changes in vegetation within the Trans-Pecos ecosystem.
The availability of water is the greatest limiting factor in the
Chihuahuan Desert, and the distribution of birds here will fluctuate
with seasonal rainfall.

Even though the Trans-Pecos area is landlocked and the water
limited, the variety of bird life is quite wide and is not relegated to
passerines. At least 39 species of shorebirds have been recorded from
the area. Of the 16 species of hummingbirds that nest in the United
States, 14 of them have been seen in the Trans-Pecos. Western and
Clark's grebes are fairly common on Lake Balmorhea, and certain
rails can be found in the cattails along the Rio Grande. Herons frequent the lakes and waterways in summer, as do ducks in winter. In
all, 483 species have been documented within the Trans-Pecos
boundaries outlined in this book. This list is larger than most state
lists and currently includes nearly four-fifths of all bird species
recorded in Texas (605 at this writing).

The Rio Grande (including its tributaries) and the wooded mountain ranges above 5,000 ft. are the two greatest commodities that the Trans-Pecos offers to most migrating birds. The heaviest migration for shorebirds and songbirds in spring occurs from mid-April to mid-May, with species abundance generally being greater in wetter years than drier years. Although frequently less intense, there is generally some migration activity in the month of March that ranges across several different bird families.

There occasionally is a second movement of birds which may occur in late summer (not fall migration) that coincides with the wet season rainfall. Resident species that are particular about nesting during the wet season include Black-chinned Sparrow and Cassin's Sparrow.

Fall migration for songbirds is somewhat scattered, ranging from mid-July for some warblers, shorebirds, and hummingbirds to late November for some sparrows. Migration for birds such as the ducks and hawks has a slightly different time frame. During fall migration, these birds arrive in the Trans-Pecos in mass a bit later than the migrating songbirds. With a few exceptions, late October and November is when most wintering hawks and waterfowl arrive in the Trans-Pecos. In spring, the migratory hawks that move through generally arrive between mid-March and mid-April. Wintering waterfowl, on the other hand, may leave in spring as early as February if weather conditions are right.

Hummingbirds show a wider range of migratory movement than most songbirds. Their food source may be feast or famine depending on rainfall and the availability of insects and flowering plants. The midsummer rains in the Trans-Pecos (or lack thereof) may determine what flowering plants are available and whether these birds can remain throughout the summer. Furthermore, climatic conditions outside the Trans-Pecos may cause detours or delays in migratory routes, making hummingbird migration as a whole somewhat sporadic.

Typically, spring migration for hummingbirds begins in March and lasts at least through late April. Fall migration may actually begin by mid-July and last until late September. Hummingbird migration will become a small trickle by mid-October. Any hummingbird seen in midwinter other than Anna's Hummingbird would be a true rarity, but occasionally a casual Rufous or Black-chinned hummingbird has been found around the winter's edge in November or February.

TAXONOMY

This annotated list of bird species follows the American Ornithologists' Union's (A.O.U.) Checklist of North American Birds, sixth edition (1983), as currently supplemented. Also, recent studies in DNA testing are mentioned in this work when the authors believe these studies to be pertinent to possible taxonomic changes in future A.O.U. supplements. The mention of DNA studies, however, does not necessarily reflect an endorsement of taxonomic changes by the authors. Since DNA studies to date have not been definitive, those changes will continue to be determined by researchers and taxonomists. The authors do, however, believe that the merit of DNA testing is so significant that it will likely have some impact on future A.O.U. supplements.

DOCUMENTATION

By definition, usage of words such as "sighting," "report," and "observation" refers to the simple passing of recorded information. However, the use of the word "record" in this instance refers to documentation that has been subjected to review by the Texas Bird Records Committee (TBRC), or has been screened by the Texas regional editors of *American Birds* magazine (now *Field Notes*), or both. Documentation of a record may include written information, tape recordings, photographs, or some combination thereof.

The TBRC is a standing committee of the Texas Ornithological Society. The TBRC is responsible for the official list of bird species for the state of Texas as compiled in the Texas Ornithological Society's *The T.O.S. Checklist of the Birds of Texas*. This official list is reviewed and updated periodically.

The term "historical record" generally refers to information which was reviewed and cited by Dr. Harry Oberholser for the book *The Bird Life of Texas*, which was published in 1974. This book may be the most exhaustive and comprehensive work on the avifauna of any state. There are, however, some historical records that Dr. Oberholser reviewed that have now become suspect because of missing documentation or specimens. Furthermore, ornithology has made so many changes in taxonomy since 1974 that certain species accounts in *The Bird Life of Texas* have been rendered out-of-date. Overall, however, *The Bird Life of Texas* clearly remains the most important reference in Texas ornithology and should be required reading for anyone interested in the state's avifauna.

In *Birds of the Trans-Pecos*, the use of the acronym "TPRF" followed by a catalog number and date refers to the "Texas Photo Records File," currently housed and managed at Texas A&M University in College Station, Texas. These photo records are exclusively of birds and are used as a visual resource for the Texas Bird Records Committee and other interested parties. The authors refer to the TPRF only for birds of unusual occurrence or hard-to-identify species that would be unexpected in the Trans-Pecos.

The acronym "TBSL" refers to the "Texas Bird Sounds Library," housed and managed at Sam Houston State University in Huntsville, Texas. This library contains the largest known collection of Texas bird sound recordings. Several species mentioned in *Birds of the Trans-Pecos*, such as the Gray Flycatcher, were tape-recorded for purposes of documentation. These recordings are indicated in the species accounts when sound was a primary concern for positive identification.

If the words *"Review Species"* are written at the end of a species account, then documentation is sought by the TBRC for any record of that species. Documentation also is requested when an accepted species, such as the Roseate Spoonbill, is seen far out of its normal range or when a species is considered casual or accidental for the area. For people with a computer and Internet access, an updated list of Texas review species can be found at the TBRC Web page. With the use of a Web browser such as Netscape or Microsoft Internet Explorer, one can visit this page using a search engine and entering keywords such as "Texas Bird Records Committee" or "TBRC."

The authors of *Birds of the Trans-Pecos* include sightings of "review species" if, and only if, at least one documented record of that species exists for the Trans-Pecos. For example, a review species may be considered in some publications to be a Trans-Pecos vagrant and will be on the official list of Texas birds. However, if the accepted documented records reviewed by the TBRC are from South Texas and not the Trans-Pecos, then we do not list it as a Trans-Pecos bird.

There is, however, one account of a review species that made this Trans-Pecos list that was never reviewed by the TBRC. Masked Duck was reported prior to the formation of the TBRC and was a multi-observer sighting that included written documentation. This documentation was lost before becoming available for review. The authors of *Birds of the Trans-Pecos* believe this sighting to be accurate and have made an exception to include it here.

The Texas Bird Records Committee also recognizes a "Presumptive List" of Texas birds. The Presumptive List is the official TBRC list of species for which written descriptions of sight records have been accepted by the TBRC, but other requirements for full acceptance (specimen, photo, video, or audio recording for at least one record) have not yet been met. Some bird record committees, including Texas', keep their Presumptive List separate from their official state checklist. The authors of this book have included all presumptive species appropriate to the Trans-Pecos in the main checklist. At present, only Crescent-chested Warbler falls into this category.

For unique Trans-Pecos birds that are not subject to review by the TBRC, i.e., Black Skimmer, the authors have used *American Birds* magazine, Roland H. Wauer's *A Field Guide to Birds of the Big Bend*, and other published and unpublished material. However, the authors have not relied solely on any preexisting material. There are published reports from several sources (including both of the sources previously mentioned) that we feel are lacking documentation and therefore did not include in this book. The species accounts in *Birds of the Trans-Pecos* have generally come from at least two (and usually three or more) respected sources. Christmas Bird Count information was used cautiously. Notes written long after the sighting and reports by a single observer were eliminated in most cases.

Because of this editing process, there are likely many valid sightings that have not been included in this book. Many of the reports of rare birds that are not "accepted" are reports that were not submitted to any *American Birds* (now *Field Notes*) magazine editor and may have been written prior to the adoption of evaluation standards by the TBRC. Some prior records simply did not have enough documentation. A vast majority of the unaccepted observations would have been better documented if the observers had known what was needed and where to send the reports. For whatever reason, there are most certainly valid sightings (some by the authors themselves) that are considered unaccepted records and are not in this book.

Of the 483 species recorded in the Trans-Pecos, 71 (15%) are considered species of "accidental" occurrence (having three or fewer reviewed records), a circumstance making the documentation and review of Trans-Pecos birds extremely difficult. When one adds a low-density human population, a close proximity to Mexico, and a wide geographical diversity, the proper documentation of birds becomes a Herculean task. Because of this frontier environment, many rumors and misidentified birds became published reports before they were properly reviewed. Other sightings "died on the vine" or went completely unreported. It is for this reason that the authors have gone to such pains to report exact dates on species of accidental occurrence. Unusual bird sightings are not at all unusual for this very special piece of the American West.

Those who believe they have seen a Trans-Pecos rarity or a state rarity may submit their documentation, preferably with a photograph, to the TBRC c/o Greg Lasley, 305 Loganberry Ct., Austin, TX 78745-6527. As stated above, the TBRC has an Internet Web page, and there are Texas rarity report forms ready to download or print out.

ABUNDANCE SCALE

The authors understand the difficulty of attempting to force a species into a definitive overall status. Whenever relevant, we have pointed to the associated habitat when referring to a bird's distribution. It is important for the reader to do likewise, and to mentally underline the phrase "in the proper habitat" when referring to words like "common" and "uncommon."

Readers should also note that seasonal notations are to be considered general in nature. For example, "fall migrants" may, in actuality, be migrating through in the summer months of July and early August, and some swallows migrating in spring may arrive in mid-to-late February. Different families, even individual species within a family, will vary greatly in the precise time and duration of their migration. For more details concerning the seasonal movements of a particular species, see the chart "The Seasonal Distribution of Trans-Pecos Birds" beginning on page 128.

The following abundance scale will be used for *Birds of the Trans-Pecos.*

Abundant	Should see on every trip in the proper habitat.
Common	Should see on 3 out of 4 trips in the proper habitat.
Fairly Common	Should see on 2 out of 4 trips in the proper habitat.
Uncommon	Should see on 1 out of 4 trips in the proper habitat.
Rare	Should see on 1 out of 10 trips or less in the proper habitat.
Casual	Not expected annually and includes out-of-season occurrences. Generally refers to 10 records or fewer for the region.
Accidental	Generally refers to 3 records or fewer for the region.
Irregular	Erratic and unpredictable in occurrence. Often applied to irruption-prone species such as Pinyon Jay.
Local	Not generally distributed throughout a region. May occur in small areas within a larger region, often as a result of fragmented habitat.

SEASONAL DEFINITIONS

Spring	March through May
Summer	June through Mid-August
Fall	Mid-August through Mid-November
Winter	Mid-November through February

AN ANNOTATED LIST OF SPECIES

LOONS: Family Gaviidae

Red-throated Loon *(Gavia stellata)*

Casual migrant and winter visitor. There are at least four well-documented records from Lake Balmorhea and one record from El Paso County. Three of the five records include catalogued photographs (TPRF #379, 646, 653). There are several unreviewed historical sightings. *Review Species.*

Pacific Loon *(Gavia pacifica)*

Casual migrant and winter visitor. There are three records from El Paso County, including two with photographs (TPRF #682 and 738), and several records from Lake Balmorhea. There are also one record from McNary Reservoir (Hudspeth County), one from Imperial Reservoir (Pecos County), and one from Red Bluff Lake (Reeves and Loving counties). Although documentation of this species is still requested, Pacific Loon was taken off the "review species" list in 1996.

Common Loon *(Gavia immer)*

Rare fall migrant and winter visitor to the Trans-Pecos. Most observations of this bird are from November to January.

Yellow-billed Loon *(Gavia adamsii)*

Accidental. Two records from the area. One specimen record from Lake Balmorhea (November 25–December 10, 1993), where the bird was seen by several observers until its death approximately two weeks later. Specimen at Texas A&M University. There is another documented sighting from the same lake on December 20, 1996. *Review Species.*

GREBES: Family Podicipedidae

Least Grebe *(Tachybaptus dominicus)*

Casual winter and spring visitor throughout the Trans-Pecos. Reports around Lake Amistad are not well documented, but this species may be a rare winter visitor on that lake.

Clark's Grebe

Pied-billed Grebe *(Podilymbus podiceps)*

Fairly common migrant and winter resident throughout the Trans-Pecos. Uncommon and local breeding species.

Horned Grebe *(Podiceps auritus)*

Rare spring and fall migrant in most of the Trans-Pecos. May be locally uncommon at a few larger reservoirs. Casual in midwinter.

Eared Grebe *(Podiceps nigricollis)*

Fairly common migrant and winter resident. Uncommon and very localized breeding species. Less common in all seasons in Big Bend country.

Western Grebe *(Aechmophorus occidentalis)*

Fairly common migrant and winter visitor. Irregular nesting bird. Western Grebes have mated with Clark's Grebes on two separate occasions in the Trans-Pecos (McNary Reservoir and Lake Balmorhea). Both of these pairings produced offspring. Generally more common than Clark's Grebe.

Clark's Grebe *(Aechmophorous clarkii)*

Uncommon to rare migrant and winter visitor. Irregular nester. A pair of Clark's Grebes have nested successfully on one occasion at

McNary Reservoir. There are two Trans-Pecos records of Clark's Grebes paired with Western Grebes—one at Lake Balmorhea and one at McNary Reservoir.

PELICANS: Family Pelecanidae

American White Pelican *(Pelecanus erythrorhynchos)*

Uncommon to rare migrant. Very rare and irregular in winter. This species is more commonly seen in fall migration, but there are several recent spring records, particularly in the southeastern Trans-Pecos. There is one June record for Hudspeth County.

Brown Pelican *(Pelecanus occidentalis)*

Casual visitor to the Trans-Pecos with most records in summer and fall. There are at least fourteen known records, most between 1989 and 1996 at scattered locations. One of the strangest records was a bird found dead in the road in Guadalupe Mountains National Park (February 23, 1996).

CORMORANTS: Family Phalacrocoracidae

Double-crested Cormorant *(Phalacrocorax auritus)*

Common migrant and winter resident on the larger lakes, but not generally found in Big Bend country. Rare and local breeding bird with nesting in Hudspeth and Reeves counties.

Neotropic Cormorant *(Phalacrocorax brasilianus)*

Fairly common in summer and uncommon in winter around Lake Amistad. This species also nests locally at McNary Reservoir and Fort Hancock Reservoir (both in Hudspeth County). Uncommon to rare elsewhere in the Trans-Pecos, with most sightings in spring, summer, and fall.

BITTERNS AND HERONS: Family Ardeidae

American Bittern *(Botaurus lentiginosus)*

Rare spring and fall migrant along the Rio Grande around Big Bend

National Park. Casual in winter. There appear to be fewer sightings of this species north and west toward El Paso.

Least Bittern *(Ixobrychus exilis)*

Rare and local breeding bird from April to September. Found around lakes or in marshy areas along the Rio Grande. This species may be more common than records indicate.

Great Blue Heron *(Ardea herodias)*

Common migrant and winter resident. Uncommon summer visitor with historical breeding records from El Paso County.

Great Egret *(Ardea alba)*

Uncommon visitor at all seasons. Breeding was not suspected until three nests were found for the first time in 1994 at McNary Reservoir (Hudspeth County).

Snowy Egret *(Egretta thula)*

Fairly common spring and fall migrant. Rare in winter. Localized breeding bird throughout the Trans-Pecos.

Little Blue Heron *(Egretta caerulea)*

Rare migrant and summer visitor, but no breeding records in the Trans-Pecos. Casual in winter.

Tricolored Heron *(Egretta tricolor)*

Rare visitor to the Trans-Pecos in spring, summer, and fall. Most observations are from late summer along the Rio Grande. No breeding records.

Reddish Egret *(Egretta rufescens)*

Casual visitor in spring, summer, and fall. One record from El Paso County, one from Hudspeth County, and several records from Lake Balmorhea, including the white morph of this species.

Cattle Egret *(Bubulcus ibis)*

Fairly common spring and fall migrant. Uncommon in winter. Locally common breeding bird at scattered locations throughout the Trans-Pecos. Numbers have steadily increased since the 1970's.

Green Heron *(Butorides virescens)*

Fairly common migrant and summer breeding resident. Uncommon to rare in winter. Generally found along densely vegetated canals, riverbanks, or ponds.

Black-crowned Night-Heron *(Nycticorax nycticorax)*

Fairly common migrant and uncommon breeding bird. Uncommon to rare in winter. Rare at all seasons in Big Bend country.

Yellow-crowned Night-Heron *(Nycticorax violacea)*

Casual visitor from May to October, with most observations coming from late summer.

IBISES: Family Threskiornithidae

White Ibis *(Eudocimus albus)*

Accidental. One spring record from Feather Lake (El Paso County, April 7, 1991) and one winter sighting from Big Bend National Park (February 8, 1971).

Glossy Ibis *(Plegadis falcinellus)*

Accidental. One photograph spring record from the Fort Bliss Sewage Ponds (El Paso County, TPRF #1097, April 29–May 4, 1992) and one documented sighting from Lake Balmorhea (April 29, 1997). Although the Glossy Ibis was recently removed as a review species for Texas, documentation for this bird in the Trans-Pecos is still requested.

White-faced Ibis *(Plegadis chihi)*

Fairly common migrant in spring and fall. Casual in winter. Fairly common to uncommon in summer, with a few local breeding records at scattered locations. Rare in Big Bend country.

Roseate Spoonbill *(Ajaia ajaia)*

Casual, usually in late summer or early fall. Most records are from August 14 to October 10. There is one very old historical record of a specimen collected in 1863 near Fort Stockton, Texas (Pecos County). More recently, there are one reliable summer sighting from Lake Balmorhea in 1980 shortly after Hurricane Allen and two records from Imperial Reservoir (Pecos County), including a series of observations of three to seven birds which apparently stayed from September 12 to October 6, 1994. There are also a record from the San Vicente area of Big Bend National Park (August 20, 1994) and a photograph record (August 14, 1996, TPRF #1355) of three birds from Red Bluff Reservoir (Reeves and Loving counties).

STORKS: Family Ciconiidae

Wood Stork *(Mycteria americana)*
Casual in late summer and early fall. Oberholser lists two separate records for El Paso County, one of which was a specimen (1937). Scattered sightings elsewhere.

AMERICAN VULTURES: Family Cathartidae

Black Vulture *(Coragyps atratus)*
Rare to casual in most of the Trans-Pecos. Uncommon along the Rio Grande watershed as far west as Brewster County. Although this species is locally common in all seasons in Val Verde County, it is virtually absent from the western Trans-Pecos. There are no records at all from El Paso County and only two from Hudspeth County.

Turkey Vulture *(Cathartes aura)*
Common summer resident throughout. Generally casual, or absent altogether, in winter, though seen with more regularity during that season in the southern and eastern Trans-Pecos.

SWANS, GEESE, AND DUCKS: Family Anatidae

Black-bellied Whistling-Duck *(Dendrocygna autumnalis)*
Casual straggler to much of the Trans-Pecos, with most records from late April to September. Generally absent in winter. On Lake Amistad, however, this species should be considered uncommon within that same seasonal time frame. There is one record from Lake Balmorhea (1988).

Fulvous Whistling-Duck *(Dendrocygna bicolor)*
Casual March through September. Records of this species are spotty

and infrequent. The last two recorded sightings were 1965 and 1985, both from the Davis Mountains. There is one historical record of a specimen collected in El Paso County (1940).

Greater White-fronted Goose *(Anser albifrons)*

Rare migrant and winter visitor. The Greater White-fronted Goose generally arrives earlier than other geese, with migrants arriving in early September.

Snow Goose *(Chen caerulescens)*

Uncommon migrant and winter resident. Casual straggler April through September.

Ross's Goose *(Chen rossii)*

Very uncommon to rare migrant and winter resident. Casual straggler April through September. Records include one late spring migrant at Rio Grande Village in Big Bend National Park, two birds that over-summered in El Paso County, and one winter photo record (TPRF #423) from Hudspeth County.

Canada Goose *(Branta canadensis)*

Uncommon migrant and winter resident. Rare in Big Bend country.

Tundra Swan *(Cygnus columbianus)*

Casual migrant and winter visitor. The majority of records are from El Paso County between late November and early March.

Wood Duck *(Aix sponsa)*

Locally uncommon resident along Rio Grande and other scattered localities. The population of this species has increased during the last decade in the El Paso area.

Gadwall *(Anas strepera)*

Common migrant and winter resident. Rare in summer, with no proof of breeding.

Eurasian Wigeon *(Anas penelope)*

Casual in winter and spring. There are over ten accepted records for the Trans-Pecos, all from El Paso and Hudspeth counties. Records include one specimen (1976) and several photographs from 1976 to 1996 (TPRF #656, 658, 295, 892). *Review Species.*

American Wigeon *(Anas americana)*

Common migrant and abundant winter resident. Casual in summer, with no evidence of breeding.

Mallard *(Anas platyrhynchos)*

Common to fairly common permanent resident. The vast majority of breeding birds are of the "Mexican Duck" race, where distinctive male plumage is lacking. The typical race of Mallard is mostly a wintering bird that occurs from late September through early May.

Blue-winged Teal *(Anas discors)*

Fairly common spring and fall migrant. Rare in summer, with at least two documented nest records. Although there are two winter records from El Paso County, this species is generally absent during that season.

Cinnamon Teal *(Anas cyanoptera)*

Fairly common migrant and uncommon to rare breeding bird. Rare in midwinter around El Paso, but considered uncommon at that time in the southern part of the Trans-Pecos.

Northern Shoveler *(Anas clypeata)*

Abundant migrant and winter resident in northern part of the Trans-Pecos. Less common in Big Bend country. Rare and local in summer, with some breeding records.

Northern Pintail *(Anas acuta)*

Common fall migrant and winter resident. Uncommon in spring. Rare in summer, with one documented breeding record.

Garganey *(Anas querquedula)*

Accidental. One record from Presidio County, where a male was seen for eight days (April 29–May 6, 1994) at a sewage treatment pond before it died of unknown causes. Specimen at Texas A&M University. *Review Species.*

Green-winged Teal *(Anas crecca)*

Abundant migrant and winter resident. Rare in summer. No evidence of breeding.

Canvasback *(Aythya valisineria)*

Fairly common to uncommon winter resident. Rare in migration, as most birds appear to leave early and arrive late in the Trans-Pecos. Casual in summer, and in all seasons in Big Bend country.

Redhead *(Aythya americana)*

Fairly common to uncommon migrant and winter resident. Very uncommon breeding bird. Casual in Big Bend country.

Ring-necked Duck *(Aythya collaris)*

Fairly common migrant and winter resident. Casual in summer. Rare in Big Bend country in all seasons.

Greater Scaup *(Aythya marila)*

Very rare winter visitor. One photograph record from Lake Balmorhea (TPRF #788 [1989]).

Lesser Scaup *(Aythya affinis)*

Fairly common migrant and winter resident. Casual in summer. Uncommon in Big Bend country.

Surf Scoter *(Melanitta perspicillata)*

Casual fall migrant, with most sightings from late October through early November. There are one winter record and two spring records. Recent observations are from El Paso, Brewster, Hudspeth, and Pecos counties.

White-winged Scoter *(Melanitta fusca)*

Accidental fall migrant. One record from Fort Bliss Sewage Ponds (El Paso County, October 31, 1991).

Black Scoter *(Melanitta nigra)*

Accidental fall migrant, with one winter record. Three females were observed at Fort Hancock Reservoir (Hudspeth County, October 25, 1990). There is one photograph record from Lake Balmorhea (TPRF #770, December 16, 1989).

Oldsquaw *(Clangula hyemalis)*

Casual migrant and winter visitor. Most records are from the northern Trans-Pecos and include three observations from El Paso County (December 15, 1974; April 26–May 12, 1991; and November 10–December 18, 1997) and one record from Hudspeth County (December 10, 1976).

Bufflehead *(Bucephala albeola)*

Fairly common to uncommon fall migrant and winter resident. Rare in spring. One record of a bird over-summering in 1994.

Common Goldeneye *(Bucephala clangula)*

Very uncommon to rare winter visitor from late November through March.

Barrow's Goldeneye *(Bucephala islandica)*

Accidental. One record from Tornillo, Texas (El Paso County), on December 20, 1995. A photograph of this bird has been reviewed but has yet to be catalogued. *Review Species.*

Hooded Merganser *(Lophodytes cucullatus)*

Rare but regular winter resident.

Red-breasted Merganser *(Mergus serrator)*

Uncommon in November in the northern part of the Trans-Pecos. Otherwise, a rare winter visitor throughout. Prefers larger reservoirs.

Common Merganser *(Mergus merganser)*

Uncommon winter resident in the Trans-Pecos (but occasionally in large numbers locally). Accidental in summer, with one record from Hudspeth County (August 1, 1994). This species generally prefers larger reservoirs.

Masked Duck *(Nomonyx dominicus)*

Accidental. Written documentation was submitted to a former editor of *American Birds* magazine of two males present at the Fort Bliss Sewage Ponds (El Paso County) from July 8 to 19, 1976. Unfortunately, this documentation was subsequently lost. Over twenty observers saw the birds. *Review Species.*

Ruddy Duck *(Oxyura jamaicensis)*

Fairly common migrant and winter resident. Uncommon and local breeding species. Less common in all seasons in Big Bend country.

Common Black-Hawk

HAWKS, HARRIERS, AND EAGLES: Family Accipitridae

Osprey *(Pandion haliaetus)*

Uncommon migrant throughout the Trans-Pecos. Very rare in winter.

Swallow-tailed Kite *(Elanoides forficatus)*

Accidental in summer and fall. One record near Marfa, Texas (Presidio County, October 15, 1987), and one photograph record from

Big Bend National Park (TPRF #30, August 5, 1969). Also, one sighting from Jeff Davis County (August 23–September 4, 1966).

White-tailed Kite *(Elanus leucurus)*

Casual visitor in all seasons.

Mississippi Kite *(Ictinia mississippiensis)*

Uncommon migrant in the Trans-Pecos. An uncommon and localized breeding bird in El Paso County, where the first recorded nesting was 1967. There has been a noticeable increase in the number of sightings throughout the Trans-Pecos since the 1960's.

Bald Eagle *(Haliaeetus leucocephalus)*

Rare to casual winter visitor along the Rio Grande and on large lakes and reservoirs.

Northern Harrier *(Circus cyaneus)*

Fairly common migrant and winter resident. Rare in summer. One historical nest record for Jeff Davis County.

Sharp-shinned Hawk *(Accipiter striatus)*

Fairly common migrant and winter resident. Casual summer resident at high elevations, where it has been an occasional nester in years past.

Cooper's Hawk *(Accipiter cooperi)*

Fairly common migrant and winter resident. Rare summer resident.

Northern Goshawk *(Accipiter gentilis)*

Accidental winter and spring visitor. Documentation of this review species is generally very poor, and many sightings go unreported. There are two midwinter records from Big Bend National Park (December 29–30, 1982, and January 20, 1989), and one immature bird was photographed in El Paso County (TPRF #812, November 13, 1989). *Review Species.*

Gray Hawk *(Asturina nitida)*

Uncommon to rare summer visitor along the Rio Grande in the southern part of the Trans-Pecos. There are several nest records from Big Bend National Park in the last decade, including a Red-shouldered Hawk/Gray Hawk nesting pair that produced offspring.

Apparently this species is undergoing some status change in numbers or habitat requirements, since very few sightings exist for Big Bend National Park prior to 1971 (R. H. Wauer). The only known records from north of Big Bend country are late summer sightings from the Davis Mountains (1969 and 1976) and one spring record from El Paso County.

Common Black-Hawk *(Buteogallus anthracinus)*

Rare but regular summer resident in the Davis Mountains. This species is a rare migrant in Big Bend and casual elsewhere in the Trans-Pecos, with far fewer sightings north of the Davis Mountains. At least two pairs of Common Black-Hawks have nested for several years in cottonwood trees just north of the town of Fort Davis. There are only scattered nest records in Texas outside the Davis Mountains, including one record from the Devils River in Val Verde County (1988) and one from the Glass Mountains in Brewster County (1991). The similar Zone-tailed Hawk, which is a documented cliff-nester in the Davis Mountains, prefers higher canyons for nesting than the tree-nesting Common Black-Hawk.

Harris's Hawk *(Parabuteo unicinctus)*

Locally uncommon resident. This species should be considered fairly common in Val Verde County in the southeast part of the Trans-Pecos. It is less common in El Paso and Hudspeth counties in the north and rare in the Big Bend country of southern Brewster and Presidio counties.

Red-shouldered Hawk *(Buteo lineatus)*

An uncommon permanent resident in Val Verde County and rare in Terrell County. Casual elsewhere in the Trans-Pecos. There are a few records from Big Bend National Park, including one nesting with a Gray Hawk near Santa Elena Canyon in 1989.

Broad-winged Hawk *(Buteo platypterus)*

Very rare migrant in the Trans-Pecos.

Swainson's Hawk *(Buteo swainsoni)*

Fairly common migrant and summer resident in the northern and central parts of the Trans-Pecos. Rare summer resident in Big Bend country. Absent in winter.

White-tailed Hawk *(Buteo albicaudatus)*

Accidental. One record from Santa Elena Canyon in Big Bend National Park (May 11, 1994). Reports suggest this species has visited Big Bend country in spring and summer, and there are sightings from Val Verde County but no observations elsewhere.

Zone-tailed Hawk *(Buteo albonotatus)*

Uncommon summer resident (normally March through August). Several nest records in Big Bend country west to Val Verde County

Harris's Hawk

and north to the Davis Mountains. There are a few scattered sight records for the Guadalupe Mountains, but nesting has not been confirmed in that mountain range. Oddly, there are no reliable records at any time of year for the northwest quarter of the Trans-Pecos.

Red-tailed Hawk *(Buteo jamaicensis)*

Abundant migrant and winter resident. Fairly common to uncommon breeding bird. The "Harlan's" subspecies is a very rare winter visitor November through March.

Ferruginous Hawk *(Buteo regalis)*

Uncommon winter resident from mid-October through March. Numbers fluctuate from year to year.

Rough-legged Hawk *(Buteo lagopus)*

Very rare winter visitor to the Trans-Pecos. This species is more likely seen in the open foothills or grasslands than in the dry desert shrub.

Golden Eagle *(Aquila chrysaetos)*

Uncommon permanent resident. Somewhat more common in winter. Nesting has occurred in the Chisos Mountains, near Big Bend Ranch, near Del Rio (Val Verde County), and consistently in El Paso County.

CARACARAS AND FALCONS: Family Falconidae

Crested Caracara *(Caracara plancus)*

Rare visitor in all seasons in Big Bend country from Presidio County in the west to Val Verde County in the east (where its status may be more uncommon than rare). Accidental in the central and northern parts of the Trans-Pecos.

American Kestrel *(Falco sparverius)*

Abundant to common winter resident. Fairly common to uncommon breeding bird.

Merlin *(Falco columbarius)*

Rare migrant and winter resident throughout the Trans-Pecos.

Aplomado Falcon *(Falco femoralis)*

Accidental in the Trans-Pecos. Most sightings are from the 1930's, '40's, and '50's. Because of research projects in south Texas and northern Mexico, any birds seen in the Trans-Pecos should be examined for leg bands. Since the reintroduction, the TBRC has taken Aplomado Falcon off the "review species" list because it believed sightings of wild birds would be too difficult to distinguish from released birds. However, one recent midwinter record from Valentine, Texas (of a bird that stayed for several weeks in 1991–1992), was reviewed, photographed, and accepted as a naturally occurring bird by the TBRC. A second report near Van Horn, Texas (November 12, 1996), is currently under review. Four other recent sightings from New Mexico also appear to be of wild individuals. Given the recent reports of potentially wild birds, the status of Aplomado Falcon as a "review species" may once again be reevaluated. Details will always be requested for any sighting of this bird in the Trans-Pecos.

Prairie Falcon *(Falco mexicanus)*

Uncommon migrant and winter resident. Uncommon and localized breeding species where appropriate cliff faces exist. Most often observed in agricultural lands or extensive grasslands.

Peregrine Falcon *(Falco peregrinus)*

Uncommon to rare migrant and localized summer resident. Rare winter visitor at least in El Paso and Hudspeth counties. Nests in Big Bend National Park and the Guadalupe Mountains.

PHEASANTS: Family Phasianidae

Wild Turkey *(Meleagris gallopavo)*

This species has been released in several parts of the Trans-Pecos and is presently considered an uncommon resident in Pecos, Terrell, Jeff Davis, and northern Brewster counties. Rare in Big Bend National Park. Formerly a rare resident of Culberson County (Guadalupe Mountains), but extirpated around 1907.

QUAIL: Family Odontophoridae

Montezuma Quail *(Cyrtonyx montezumae)*

Fairly common resident in the high grasslands of the Davis Mountains and a few of the smaller mountain ranges of the Trans-Pecos.
This species is not easily seen, but it does have a quiet, haunting call
that can be heard regularly in the appropriate habitat. Montezuma
Quail appear to be gone from the Chisos Mountains of the Big
Bend. They were reintroduced into the Guadalupe Mountains to the
north in 1984, but their current status there is unclear. One record
from Lake Balmorhea.

Gambel's Quail

Montezuma Quail

Northern Bobwhite *(Colinus virginianus)*

Common in the southeast part of the Trans-Pecos and rare in Reeves and Jeff Davis counties. Now generally believed to be absent in the Big Bend area and in the northern and western counties. Reintroductions have occurred in the Guadalupe Mountains and on private ranches.

Scaled Quail *(Callipepla squamata)*

Common resident in desert habitats throughout the Trans-Pecos. Numbers often decline significantly following drought years.

Gambel's Quail *(Callipepla gambelii)*

Common local resident along the Rio Grande in El Paso, Hudspeth, and northern Presidio counties and less common in the desert flats. Very rare in most of Big Bend country. Somewhat irregular (and perhaps cyclic). In the El Paso area, this species is expanding into drier desert areas formerly held by Scaled Quail.

RAILS, GALLINULES, AND COOTS: Family Rallidae

Yellow Rail *(Coturnicops noveboracensis)*

Accidental. There are two records from Big Bend National Park (January 31, 1976, and March 27, 1989). The earliest record was of an injured bird that died shortly after it was found (R. H. Wauer). Specimen in Big Bend National Park collection.

King Rail *(Rallus elegans)*

Very rare in the Trans-Pecos in summer. There are one nest record in El Paso County in 1933 and a few summer records around Big Bend National Park and Lake Balmorhea that suggest nesting. Recent documentation includes photographs (TPRF #391 and #1053) and tape recordings.

Virginia Rail *(Rallus limicola)*

Uncommon migrant and uncommon to rare summer breeding bird. Rare and local winter resident at least in El Paso and Hudspeth counties. There is one photo record from the area (TPRF #1052, Jeff Davis County, 1993). As with the previous species, this bird is likely very localized in the Trans-Pecos due to the extreme fluctuations in water levels around appropriate marsh habitat.

Sora *(Porzana carolina)*

Fairly common migrant. Uncommon winter resident. Rare and sporadic breeding species.

Purple Gallinule *(Porphyrula martinica)*

Very rare spring migrant in Big Bend country. Most observations are from Rio Grande Village in Big Bend National Park (R. H. Wauer). One specimen was taken from the Black Gap Wildlife Management Area headquarters (Brewster County) June 6, 1983, and is now at Sul Ross University.

Common Moorhen *(Gallinula chloropus)*

Fairly common permanent resident around El Paso, with a few nest records from Presidio County and elsewhere. Rare migrant in most of the Trans-Pecos.

American Coot *(Fulica americana)*

Abundant winter resident and common to fairly common breeding species in El Paso County. Decidedly less common (but still nesting) south into Big Bend country.

CRANES: Family Gruidae

Sandhill Crane *(Grus canadensis)*

Uncommon fall migrant. Rare in winter, with only one known record beyond mid-March.

PLOVERS: Family Charadriidae

Black-bellied Plover *(Pluvialis squatarola)*

Rare migrant, with most sightings occurring mid-August to late November.

American Golden-Plover *(Pluvialis dominica)*

Casual fall migrant, including four records from El Paso County, all between the dates September 3 and October 22. Accidental in spring, with one photograph record from Fort Bliss Sewage Ponds (El Paso County) on May 20, 1997.

Snowy Plover *(Charadrius alexandrinus)*

Fairly common to rare migrant and locally uncommon breeding bird. Very rare in winter. This species breeds at Lake Balmorhea, Toyah Lake (Reeves County), Imperial Reservoir (Pecos County), Red Bluff Lake (Reeves and Loving counties), and around the Lake Amistad area, where it nests with some regularity. Water levels around the lakes have a large impact on nest site availability. Generally absent in Big Bend country.

Semipalmated Plover *(Charadrius semipalmatus)*

Uncommon migrant in most of the Trans-Pecos. One winter record from Lake Balmorhea. Generally absent from Big Bend country.

Piping Plover *(Charadrius melodus)*

Accidental fall migrant. Two records from El Paso County (August 18, 1987, and September 20, 1990).

Mountain Plover

Killdeer *(Charadrius vociferus)*

Common permanent resident. Fairly common to uncommon in Big Bend country.

Mountain Plover *(Charadrius montanus)*

Currently, this bird is a very rare summer resident in the Davis Mountains grasslands. There are a few historical nest records from Big Bend country. This species is rarely seen in migration in any part of the Trans-Pecos but should be looked for at sod farms and freshly plowed fields.

AVOCETS AND STILTS: Family Recurvirostridae

Black-necked Stilt *(Himantopus mexicanus)*

Common to fairly common migrant and uncommon summer resident. This species has become an increasingly regular wintering bird in El Paso County. Rare migrant in Big Bend country.

American Avocet *(Recurvirostra americana)*

Fairly common migrant and summer resident. Casual in winter.

JACANAS: Family Jacanidae

Northern Jacana *(Jacana spinosa)*

Accidental. One photograph record from Brewster County near Marathon, Texas (TPRF #404, October 7–11, 1982). *Review Species.*

WOODCOCK, SNIPE, AND SANDPIPERS: Family Scolopacidae

Greater Yellowlegs *(Tringa melanoleuca)*

Fairly common spring and fall migrant. Uncommon wintering species. As with most shorebirds, this species could turn up anytime during the summer in migration.

Lesser Yellowlegs *(Tringa flavipes)*

Fairly common spring and fall migrant. Rare wintering bird.

Solitary Sandpiper *(Tringa solitaria)*

Fairly common to uncommon migrant throughout the Trans-Pecos.

Willet *(Catoptrophorus semipalmatus)*

Uncommon migrant in spring and rare in fall.

Spotted Sandpiper *(Actitis macularia)*

Common migrant. Fairly common wintering bird along parts of the Rio Grande, but uncommon and local in most areas at that time of year.

Upland Sandpiper *(Bartramia longicauda)*

Uncommon fall migrant (early August through early September). Spring sightings are very rare, most being in the southern and eastern parts of the Trans-Pecos. In the El Paso area, this species is seen almost exclusively in cut alfalfa fields.

Whimbrel *(Numenius phaeopus)*

Casual spring migrant. Most records are from El Paso County and include nine observations between the dates of April 9 and June 16.

Long-billed Curlew *(Numenius americanus)*

Uncommon spring and fall migrant. Rare and sporadic wintering species along the Rio Grande. There is one historical nest record from Jeff Davis County (May 15, 1936). There is also a recent record of seven birds that over-summered in El Paso in 1994, but they were not suspected of breeding.

Hudsonian Godwit *(Limosa haemastica)*

Accidental. One record from the Fort Hancock Reservoir (Hudspeth County), June 18, 1997. Oberholser lists two historical records for the Trans-Pecos (spring and summer—but the specific year was not given). One of these records was a July specimen taken from El Paso County.

Marbled Godwit *(Limosa fedoa)*

Very uncommon to rare spring migrant and rare fall migrant. Fewer sightings south into Big Bend country. One photograph record from the Fort Hancock Reservoir (Hudspeth County) on June 6, 1997.

Ruddy Turnstone *(Arenaria interpres)*

Casual spring and fall migrant. Most sightings are from El Paso and Hudspeth counties. Spring records fall between April 14 and May 8, and fall sightings are from September 20 to October 8.

Red Knot *(Calidris canutus)*

Casual spring and fall migrant. There is one spring record of eight birds observed on May 22, 1971. Fall records include individual birds seen August 1, 1984, August 24, 1985, and August 20, 1987, all from El Paso County.

Sanderling *(Calidris alba)*

Very rare fall migrant. Casual in spring, with three records from El Paso County all occurring during the month of May. In fall, this species occurs almost every year, usually from September to late October with peaks during the second and third weeks of September. Most often observed in El Paso and Hudspeth counties.

Semipalmated Sandpiper *(Calidris pusilla)*

Very uncommon to rare fall migrant. Most records are of juveniles in late August. Very rare in spring. One photograph record from Hudspeth County (TPRF #444, September 20, 1985).

Western Sandpiper *(Calidris mauri)*

Common to fairly common spring and fall migrant. Casual in midwinter.

Red-necked Stint *(Calidris ruficollis)*

Accidental in summer. There is one record from the Fort Bliss Sewage Ponds (El Paso County) from July 17 to 22, 1996. The bird was seen by an entire birding group. Photographs have been submitted but are currently uncatalogued. At this writing, this is the only record of Red-necked Stint for Texas. *Review Species.*

Least Sandpiper *(Calidris minutilla)*

Abundant to common spring and fall migrant. Fairly common wintering bird. Less common in all seasons in Big Bend country.

White-rumped Sandpiper *(Calidris fuscicollis)*

Rare spring migrant (early May–early June). Casual in fall.

Baird's Sandpiper *(Calidris bairdii)*

Uncommon migrant. More numerous in fall. Often seen away from water at places like sod farms and golf courses.

Pectoral Sandpiper *(Calidris melanotos)*

Rare spring migrant. Uncommon in fall. Most often seen mid-September to mid-October.

Dunlin *(Calidris alpina)*

Very rare fall migrant and winter visitor. Most records are from El Paso and Hudspeth counties in October and November.

Stilt Sandpiper *(Calidris himantopus)*

Rare spring migrant. Fairly common in fall in the El Paso area, but few observations elsewhere in that season.

Ruff *(Philomachus pugnax)*

Accidental. One accepted record from Fort Bliss Sewage Ponds (El Paso County, September 5–11, 1993). *Review Species.*

Short-billed Dowitcher *(Limnodromus griseus)*

Rare fall migrant. One photograph record from Hudspeth County (TPRF #441 [1985]).

Long-billed Dowitcher *(Limnodromus scolopaceus)*

Fairly common migrant. Uncommon winter resident. Rare in Big Bend country.

Common Snipe *(Gallinago gallinago)*

Fairly common to uncommon migrant and winter resident.

American Woodcock *(Scolopax minor)*

Casual fall migrant. Accidental in winter, where there are at least three records. One bird was photographed in El Paso, December 27, 1984, and a specimen record exists from El Paso from January 25, 1995 (specimen at University of Texas–El Paso). There is a third winter record from the Devils River State Natural Area (Val Verde County), February 22, 1996. There are several fall sightings from Big Bend National Park.

Wilson's Phalarope *(Phalaropus tricolor)*

Common to fairly common migrant. Early and late migrants can be seen throughout the summer. Uncommon in Big Bend country. One winter record for El Paso County (December 4, 1985).

Red-necked Phalarope *(Phalaropus lobatus)*

Casual spring migrant and uncommon fall migrant (late August through late October). It should be noted that nearly all records of Red-necked Phalarope (and Red Phalarope) are from El Paso and Hudspeth counties.

Red Phalarope *(Phalaropus fulicaria)*

Casual fall migrant around the El Paso area. There are four documented sightings ranging from September 17 through October 28. Two of these sightings include photograph records (TPRF #953 and #990), and there is one specimen record currently at Texas A&M University. Also, one unreviewed sighting at Lake Balmorhea (1990). *Review Species.*

GULLS, KITTIWAKES, AND TERNS: Family Laridae

Parasitic Jaeger *(Stercorarius parasiticus)*

Accidental. One fall record of two indivuduals from Red Bluff Lake (Reeves and Loving counties, November 28, 1991).

Long-tailed Jaeger *(Stercorarius longicaudus)*

Accidental. One summer record (June 12–14, 1996) of a single individual from McNary Reservoir (Hudspeth County). Photographs exist but have not been catalogued at this writing. *Review Species.*

Laughing Gull *(Larus atricilla)*

Rare spring, summer, and fall visitor to the Trans-Pecos. This species has nested at Lake Amistad (as of 1995), and the status of this coastal species may be changing, as it has turned up at inland locations throughout Texas with much more regularity in the last decade. Two photo records from the area (TPRF #447 and #1063).

Franklin's Gull *(Larus pipixcan)*

Fairly common to uncommon spring migrant and rare fall migrant. Casual in winter and a casual straggler in summer (occasionally staying throughout the summer, but no nest records). Very rare as a migrant in Big Bend country.

Bonaparte's Gull *(Larus philadelphia)*

Uncommon fall migrant. Rare in midwinter and spring throughout the Trans-Pecos.

Mew Gull *(Larus canus)*

Accidental. Two winter records from Hudspeth County (January 1– February 13, 1988, and January 26, 1993) and one from El Paso County (January 21, 1998). All records were photographed—one catalogued (TPRF #634 [1988]). *Review Species.*

Ring-billed Gull *(Larus delawarensis)*

Fairly common migrant and winter resident. Very rare straggler in summer. Rare in Big Bend country.

California Gull *(Larus californicus)*

Casual visitor, with seven scattered records from El Paso and Hudspeth counties and three additional sightings from that area which appear to be good but remain unsubmitted for review. One documented record from Lake Balmorhea on April 29, 1997. Most records range from November 5 through May 26. Perhaps the best documented record is of a first summer bird that stayed from June 12 to August 2, 1996 (Hudspeth County). Photograph records for the Trans-Pecos include TPRF#635 and #991. *Review Species.*

Herring Gull *(Larus argentatus)*

Rare but regular winter visitor to the Trans-Pecos from October through March. Hypothetical around Big Bend National Park.

Thayer's Gull *(Larus thayeri)*

Accidental. One first-year bird at Fort Hancock Reservoir (Hudspeth County) was reported with written details in 1984 (although the documentation remains unsubmitted to the TBRC). A photograph record from El Paso County was recently submitted for review (January 28, 1997). This bird may undergo a change in regard to its species status. Recent evidence suggests a single species of Iceland Gull in which *L. glaucoides glaucoides* is generally found on the east coast, *L. g. kumlieni* in central North America, and *L. g. thayeri* on the west coast. If Iceland Gull becomes the accepted species, it will replace Thayer's Gull on this list. *Review Species.*

Lesser Black-backed Gull *(Larus fuscus)*

Accidental. One fall photograph record from Lake Balmorhea (TPRF #985, November 29–December 3, 1990), and a second unreviewed sighting from that lake in mid-November of 1991. A photograph record from El Paso County has recently been submitted for review (January 28, 1997). *Review Species.*

Western Gull *(Larus occidentalis)*

Accidental. One bird photographed at Fort Bliss Sewage Ponds (El Paso County, TPRF #514, May 14, 1986). This record is the first of only two Western Gull records for Texas. *Review Species.*

Black-legged Kittiwake *(Rissa tridactyla)*

Casual. Five Trans-Pecos records, all from the 1990's; all sightings from mid-November through December. Records are from El Paso and Hudspeth counties, Lake Balmorhea, Imperial Reservoir in Pecos County, and Red Bluff Lake in Reeves and Loving counties. *Review Species.*

Sabine's Gull *(Xema sabini)*

Casual fall visitor. Accidental in spring and summer. In the fall of 1988, there were three Trans-Pecos records in one month's time. Nearly all records for the Trans-Pecos range from September 6 to October 7. There are one spring record from McNary Reservoir (Hudspeth County) from May 6, 1995, and a summer record from the same location July 13–15, 1996. Both McNary Reservoir records were documented with photos and are currently under review by the TBRC. *Review Species.*

Caspian Tern *(Sterna caspia)*

Casual visitor. Most records from summer and fall (June 15 through October 6) from the northern Trans-Pecos.

Elegant Tern *(Sterna elegans)*

Accidental. One photograph record from Lake Balmorhea (TPRF #397, December 23, 1987). *Review Species.*

Common Tern *(Sterna hirundo)*

Rare migrant. Most likely observed in fall migration. Records from El Paso and Hudspeth counties (1984 and 1985) contain photographs (TPRF #449 and #450).

Arctic Tern *(Sterna paradisaea)*

One record (the first Texas record) from McNary Reservoir in Hudspeth County (June 5–6, 1997). This bird was observed feeding at the reservoir for at least two days. It was photographed by two different observers (photographs uncatalogued). *Review Species.*

Forster's Tern *(Sterna forsteri)*

Fairly common spring and fall migrant on lakes and reservoirs. Rare migrant in Big Bend country. Casual in winter.

Least Tern *(Sterna antillarium)*

Rare migrant and locally uncommon breeding bird at lakes and reservoirs. This species has nested near Lake Amistad in sandbar habitat with Snowy Plovers and Black-necked Stilts. There are no known studies to show whether the nesting birds near Lake Amistad are the inland nesting and endangered *S. a. athalassos* subspecies or the coastal *S. a. antillarium.* The more common coastal subspecies has been known to nest inland, migrating from the coast up the Rio Grande to nest in southwest Texas.

Sooty Tern *(Sterna fuscata)*

Accidental. One summer record of three birds blown in by Hurricane Allen. Two were found in Brewster County and one in Jeff Davis County (August 12, 1980). All of the birds were found dead or died shortly thereafter. One specimen is currently at Sul Ross University.

Black Tern *(Chlidonias niger)*

Uncommon to fairly common migrant. Very rare in Big Bend country.

Black Skimmer *(Rynchops niger)*

Accidental. One summer record from Lake Balmorhea August 12, 1980, after Hurricane Allen (photograph, TPRF #216).

PIGEONS AND DOVES: Family Columbidae

Rock Dove *(Columba livia)*

Abundant in urban centers like El Paso. Uncommon and local in small towns and rare elsewhere.

Band-tailed Pigeon *(Columba fasciata)*

Fairly common summer resident. Uncommon and sporadic in winter. Generally found in the montane habitat of the Davis and Chisos mountains and perhaps some of the smaller mountain ranges. Casual in other parts of the Trans-Pecos. These birds are known to travel widely and frequent fruiting mulberry trees or oak trees with good acorn crops.

White-winged Dove *(Zenaida asiatica)*

Common to fairly common summer resident. Uncommon and localized in winter, although large numbers can still be found in residential areas of El Paso in that season.

Mourning Dove *(Zenaida macroura)*

Abundant to common summer resident and common to fairly common in winter.

Inca Dove *(Scardafella inca)*

Locally fairly common permanent resident, particularly in city suburbs. Less common outside of parks and residential areas.

Common Ground-Dove *(Columbina passerina)*

Accidental in all seasons except in Presidio, Brewster, and Terrell counties, where it is an uncommon to very rare permanent resident. There is one fall record from Hueco Tanks State Park. Most records from the northern Trans-Pecos are from March to October.

Ruddy Ground-Dove *(Columbina talpacoti)*

Casual. Two well-documented winter records from Big Bend National Park (December 12, 1987–early May 1988, and December 24, 1991–May 5, 1992), one record near Lajitas, Texas (Brewster County, February 22–March 22, 1990), and one record of two birds in El Paso (April 20–23, 1996). Records with photographs include TPRF #602 and #870. *Review Species.*

White-tipped Dove *(Leptotila verreauxi)*

Accidental. One documented record (TPRF #220, October 17, 1989) from Dolan Creek in Val Verde County and two summer sightings from Big Bend National Park (R. H. Wauer). Although this species is fairly common in south Texas, there are very few records for the Trans-Pecos.

PARROTS: Family Psittacidae

Monk Parakeet *(Myiopsitta monachus)*

Locally uncommon. A small but growing population in El Paso has been present there for over a decade.

CUCKOOS, ROADRUNNERS, AND ANIS: Family Cuculidae

Black-billed Cuckoo *(Coccyzus erythropthalmus)*

Accidental in the Trans-Pecos. One reliable fall sighting in the Davis Mountains (September 9, 1991) and a few hypothetical sightings from Big Bend National Park. Although two local checklists show this bird as a rare, regular migrant, there is little documentation to support it.

Yellow-billed Cuckoo *(Coccyzus americanus)*

Fairly common to uncommon summer resident. Late spring migrant (usually mid-May). Frequently inhabits cottonwoods and salt cedar bosques. May be declining in El Paso County as habitat declines.

Greater Roadrunner *(Geococcyx californianus)*

Fairly common resident up to about 5,500 ft.

Groove-billed Ani *(Crotophaga sulcirostris)*

Fairly common resident in spring and summer around the Del Rio area (Val Verde County). Rare visitor in spring and summer in Big Bend country. Casual at all seasons north of the Big Bend, with only two records from the El Paso area.

BARN OWLS: Family Tytonidae

Barn Owl *(Tyto alba)*

Fairly common to uncommon permanent resident in the El Paso area. The status of this bird in the rest of the Trans-Pecos is somewhat sketchy. Wauer considered this species a rare migrant in Big Bend National Park, and it is likely a rare visitor, perhaps nesting, in other areas.

TYPICAL OWLS: Family Strigidae

Flammulated Owl *(Otus flammeolus)*

Fairly common to uncommon migrant and summer resident in montane forests, usually above 6,000 ft. Rare spring and fall migrant in lowland areas. Most observations are from Boot Spring in the Chisos Mountains, near the top of Mt. Livermore in the Davis Mountains, and from Dog Canyon and The Bowl high in the Guadalupe Mountains.

Eastern Screech-Owl *(Otus asio)*

Uncommon to rare permanent resident in the southern and eastern sections of the Trans-Pecos. Absent from El Paso and Hudspeth counties in the north and west. Separated from Western Screech-Owl by voice and bill color.

Western Screech-Owl *(Otus kennicottii)*

Common to fairly common permanent resident. Rare in El Paso and Hudspeth counties. There is some range overlap with the previous species in the southern and eastern parts of the range. Generally more common than the Eastern Screech-Owl where ranges overlap.

Great Horned Owl *(Bubo virginianus)*

Fairly common permanent resident throughout the Trans-Pecos.

Northern Pygmy Owl *(Glaucidium gnoma)*

There are only two accepted records of this species in Texas, both from Boot Spring in Big Bend National Park (August 12, 1982, and April 25, 1993). However, the many unsubmitted reports indicate that this bird is likely a casual migrant and summer visitor to the Trans-Pecos, perhaps even nesting. There are several summer reports of vocalizations by this species (those of other birds and even Rock Squirrels are similar) in the montane habitat of all three major mountain ranges. Most reports are unsubmitted for review or unaccepted for lack of any visual identification. Wauer lists five sightings (unsubmitted for review) for Big Bend National Park. There is one historical record of a specimen collected in El Paso (1918). *Review Species.*

Elf Owl *(Micrathene whitneyi)*

Common to fairly common migrant and summer resident (March through September) in much of Big Bend country, particularly along the Rio Grande and into Val Verde County. Less common north to Jeff Davis County, where records are scattered. Accidental in winter and in the northern half of the Trans-Pecos.

Burrowing Owl *(Athene cunicularia)*

Locally fairly common throughout much of the Trans-Pecos grasslands. Seen more frequently in the northwest edge of the state from northern Presidio County to El Paso County. Much less common in winter. Very rare in Big Bend National Park.

Spotted Owl *(Strix occidentalis)*

Rare and local permanent resident. There is one documented nest record from the Davis Mountains, but only one other sighting in that mountain range in over a decade (August 2, 1997). There are infrequent sight records, some of paired birds, from the Guadalupe Mountains where it is presumed to nest. There are three records from El Paso County, all with photographs. One El Paso record is of a specimen found dead (TPRF #641, November 3, 1985). No records at all from Big Bend country.

Barred Owl *(Strix varia)*

Uncommon permanent resident around wet, low-lying areas in Val Verde County. Generally absent elsewhere.

Long-eared Owl *(Asio otus)*

Uncommon to rare migrant and winter resident and occasional nester. Very irregular in all seasons. As many as six have been seen at Hueco Tanks State Park in winter, but this bird is not reliably seen at any one location. One nest record from Jeff Davis County (1991). Oberholser also lists one historic breeding record from El Paso County (1918). There are two June sightings (1967 and 1970) from Boot Spring in the Chisos Mountains (R. H. Wauer), but no evidence of nesting was ever found in that mountain range.

Short-eared Owl *(Asio flammeus)*

Casual migrant and winter visitor. Most sightings are from November through March. In the 1970's, this species was regular in very small numbers in El Paso County, but there have been no reliable sightings there since 1984.

Northern Saw-whet Owl *(Aegolius acadicus)*

Casual migrant and winter visitor throughout. An apparent summer resident in coniferous forests above 6,000 ft. in the Guadalupe and Davis mountains. One winter record from Big Bend National Park. Although this bird is presumed to be a local summer resident, it should be considered a low-density species within the limited, high-elevation habitat in the Trans-Pecos. There are currently only seven accepted Texas records. *Review Species.*

NIGHTHAWKS: Family Caprimulgidae

Lesser Nighthawk *(Chordeiles acutipennis)*

Common migrant and summer resident April through August. Uncommon September through October. Very rare in winter.

Common Nighthawk *(Chordeiles minor)*

Uncommon migrant and local breeding bird. Nesting occurs in the Davis Mountains, Guadalupe Mountains, and perhaps some of the smaller mountain ranges.

Pauraque *(Nyctidromus albicollis)*

Accidental. One record of two birds calling in Del Rio, Texas (May 9–29, 1987, Val Verde County), which would likely be the northernmost limit of their range.

Common Poorwill *(Phalaenoptilus nuttallii)*

Common to fairly common migrant and summer resident. Because of its strange cold-weather habit of hibernation, the status of this bird in winter is not entirely clear. There is one December record of a hibernating bird found in someone's fireplace!

Chuck-will's-widow *(Caprimulgus carolinensis)*

Accidental. One record from Devils River State Natural Area in Val Verde County (September 11, 1996).

Whip-poor-will *(Caprimulgus vociferus)*

Common to fairly common migrant and summer resident at elevations above 5,500 ft. in most of the Trans-Pecos mountains. Accidental migrant in El Paso County.

SWIFTS: Family Apodidae

Chimney Swift *(Chaetura pelagica)*

Common migrant and summer resident only around Del Rio (Val Verde County). In the 1990's, however, this species was documented nesting locally in Alpine, Texas (Brewster County) and in the town of Fort Davis, where at least one pair nested. Casual elsewhere in the Trans-Pecos.

White-throated Swift *(Aeronautes saxatalis)*

Common to fairly common migrant and summer resident. Uncommon in winter.

HUMMINGBIRDS: Family Trochilidae

Broad-billed Hummingbird *(Cynanthus latirostris)*

Casual at all seasons, with scattered records throughout. There are some historical nest records from the 1930's and 1940's in Big Bend country, but no nesting has occurred recently. *Review Species.*

White-eared Hummingbird *(Hylocharis leucotis)*

Casual spring and summer visitor. There are two fall records. Most sightings are of stragglers, with records from El Paso, Guadalupe Mountains National Park, and Big Bend National Park. There have been recent records of birds in the Davis Mountains appearing throughout the summer, which may suggest breeding in that mountain range. *Review Species.*

Berylline Hummingbird *(Amazilia beryllina)*

Accidental. There are two accepted sight records in the Trans-Pecos. The first sighting was from Big Bend National Park (August 18, 1991). This record contained only written details, and the bird was put on the Texas "Presumptive List." Six years later a Berylline Hummingbird was recorded coming to a feeder in the Davis Mountains (August 17–September 4, 1997). This second record included photographs (as yet uncatalogued) and established this species on the official list of Texas birds. *Review Species.*

Violet-crowned Hummingbird *(Amazilia violiceps)*

Accidental. There are three accepted records. The first documented Texas record was at a feeder in El Paso (TPRF #594, December 2–14, 1987), the second was near Boquillas Canyon in Big Bend National Park (March 30–31, 1996), and the third at a feeder in Val Verde County (October 31, 1996). *Review Species.*

Blue-throated Hummingbird *(Lampornis clemenciae)*

Fairly common migrant and summer resident in Big Bend country, but decidedly less common farther north. At least one nest record from the Guadalupe Mountains. Accidental in El Paso County.

Magnificent Hummingbird *(Eugenes fulgens)*

Uncommon and local summer resident (March through August) in high mountain woodlands throughout the Trans-Pecos. Very rare outside the mountain ranges and in other seasons.

Lucifer Hummingbird *(Calothorax lucifer)*

Somewhat irregular but locally fairly common resident in Big Bend country from March through early November. Rare to casual elsewhere in the Trans-Pecos. There are an increasing number of records from the Davis Mountains, but nesting there has not been confirmed. A pair was also observed in Guadalupe Mountains National Park on May 30, 1996.

Ruby-throated Hummingbird *(Archilochus colubris)*

Very rare spring, summer, and fall straggler to the Trans-Pecos. Most sightings are from Big Bend National Park and the Davis Mountains.

Black-chinned Hummingbird *(Archilochus alexandri)*

Common summer resident, generally seen from March through October. Casual in winter, with relatively few December records, none for January, and only one for February.

Anna's Hummingbird *(Calypte anna)*

Uncommon to rare fall and winter visitor throughout the Trans-Pecos. Casual in summer, with the only Texas nest record occurring in Jeff Davis County (TPRF #101, April 17–20, 1976). This may be the farthest east that this species has ever nested in the United States. Although rare, Anna's Hummingbird is the Trans-Pecos hummingbird most likely to be seen in midwinter.

Costa's Hummingbird *(Calypte costae)*

Casual. There are now several documented records from El Paso County, most from the 1990's and nearly all at feeders. There are one record with a submitted photograph (TPRF #71, March 8–28, 1975), one with a tape recording (TBSL #203-15, September 16–17,

1992), and several records under review with photographs. One record is of four to six individuals that were observed between October 26 and December 11, 1995. There are several sightings from Big Bend National Park. *Review Species.*

Calliope Hummingbird *(Stellula calliope)*

Uncommon to rare migrant (July through September). There is one photograph record of an immature male wintering in El Paso during the winter of 1995–1996 and a second winter record from the same feeder in 1997–1998. The most likely place to observe Calliope Hummingbird in Texas appears to be the Franklin Mountains, where in late summer more than a dozen have been seen in one day.

Broad-tailed Hummingbird *(Selasphorus platycercus)*

Fairly common to uncommon migrant throughout the Trans-Pecos and common to uncommon summer resident in the high country. There are two winter records for El Paso County. This species is frequently seen in oak-juniper woodlands and coniferous forests.

Rufous Hummingbird *(Selasphorus rufus)*

Common in late summer and fall until mid-October. Casual in spring and winter.

Allen's Hummingbird *(Selasphorus sasin)*

Accidental. There is only one accepted record of this bird in the Trans-Pecos. A fully gorgeted adult male was observed at a feeder in the Davis Mountains (July 26–August 5, 1994). Because of the confusion of this species and "green-backed" Rufous Hummingbirds, a few Trans-Pecos sightings of Allen's Hummingbird have not been accepted. The Texas Bird Records Committee correctly handles such observations with some conservatism. Birders should be cautious as well, and documentation sent to the TBRC should be thorough. *Review Species.*

TROGONS: Family Trogonidae

Elegant Trogon *(Trogon elegans)*

Accidental. One accepted spring record (April 29, 1993) and a few unsubmitted sightings, all from Big Bend National Park. *Review Species.*

KINGFISHERS: Family Alcedinidae

Ringed Kingfisher *(Ceryle torquata)*

Uncommon along streams and rivers in southern Val Verde County near Del Rio where it apparently nests. Records also exist at Independence Creek (Terrell County) and Dolan falls (Val Verde County). Generally absent in most of the Trans-Pecos.

Belted Kingfisher *(Ceryle alcyon)*

Fairly common migrant and winter resident. Rare in summer, possibly nesting in El Paso and Hudspeth counties but not yet confirmed.

Green Kingfisher *(Chloroceryle americana)*

Fairly common in all seasons around Lake Amistad. Rare migrant and summer visitor along Independence Creek in Terrell County west to Big Bend National Park. One photograph record (TPRF #1354) from that park on August 18, 1996. Casual elsewhere in the Trans-Pecos.

WOODPECKERS: Family Picidae

Lewis's Woodpecker *(Melanerpes lewis)*

Casual, with fall, winter, and spring sightings. An invasion winter in 1989–1990 brought five records to the Trans-Pecos ranging from December 16 to May 9. Birds were documented in El Paso in the fall and winter of 1995–1996 and again in 1996–1997. This species has been seen in both high coniferous forests and in large cottonwoods along washes and streambeds, and even in residential neighborhoods at low elevations. *Review Species.*

Red-headed Woodpecker *(Melanerpes erythrocephalus)*

Casual in the Trans-Pecos. Sightings in Brewster County are mostly from spring and summer. There are two El Paso records (October 17–19, 1982, and May 17–July 18, 1992). There is one winter sighting from Guadalupe Mountains National Park.

Acorn Woodpecker *(Melanerpes formicivorus)*

Common resident in the Chisos, Davis, and Guadalupe mountains, usually above 4,000 ft. Rare at lower elevations in fall and winter.

Acorn Woodpecker

Golden-fronted Woodpecker *(Melanerpes aurifrons)*

Common in Val Verde County and less common along the Rio Grande floodplain to Big Bend National Park and west into Presidio County. Casual in the northern half of the Trans-Pecos, with no records at all from El Paso or Hudspeth counties.

Yellow-bellied Sapsucker *(Sphyrapicus varius)*

Uncommon to rare migrant and winter resident throughout the Trans-Pecos. Less commonly seen than the Red-naped Sapsucker.

Red-naped Sapsucker *(Sphyrapicus nuchalis)*

Uncommon migrant and winter resident. There are records from high-elevation forests to low-elevation pecan groves and residential areas. Most records are from fall and winter. Some reports suggest nesting in the Guadalupe Mountains, but the authors have seen no clear documentation of breeding.

Williamson's Sapsucker *(Sphyrapicus thyroideus)*

Very rare migrant and winter visitor. There are sporadic sightings of this species through most of the Trans-Pecos. However, this sapsucker is seen uncommonly but regularly during the winter in the high coniferous forests of the Davis Mountains.

Ladder-backed Woodpecker *(Picoides scalaris)*

Common to fairly common permanent resident. This species is found in a variety of habitats from mesquite brushland to riparian to oak-juniper foothills.

Downy Woodpecker *(Picoides pubescens)*

Very rare in fall, winter, and spring. There are three records from El Paso County and several reports from the Guadalupe Mountains.

Hairy Woodpecker *(Picoides villosus)*

Accidental in most of the Trans-Pecos, but considered an uncommon permanent resident in the Guadalupe Mountains. Two documented records from El Paso County.

Northern Flicker *(Colaptes auratus)*

The "Red-shafted" Flicker *(C. auratus collaris)* is a common migrant and winter resident. It is a fairly common breeding bird, being more common in the high country where it prefers to nest. The "Yellow-shafted" Flicker *(C. a. luteus)* is a rare migrant and winter resident. A Mexican form of the "Red-shafted" Flicker *(C. a. nanus)* is an uncommon resident in the Chisos Mountains.

FLYCATCHERS: Family Tyrannidae

Tufted Flycatcher *(Mitrephanes phaeocercus)*

Accidental. The two records for the region currently represent the only known occurrence of this species in the United States. The first record was a bird discovered at Rio Grande Village in Big Bend National Park and was seen from November 3, 1991 to January 17, 1992. A second bird was discovered at an Interstate 10 roadside park in Pecos County and was observed April 2–5, 1993. *Review Species.*

Olive-sided Flycatcher *(Contopus cooperi)*

Uncommon migrant. Very uncommon to rare summer resident at very high elevations. Nesting generally occurs above 7,500 ft. in the Guadalupe Mountains and, less commonly and perhaps irregularly, in the Davis Mountains.

Greater Pewee *(Contopus pertinax)*

Accidental. There are three accepted Trans-Pecos records. A lone bird was seen in Boot Canyon in the Chisos Mountains on August 17, 1991, and there is a second report from the Davis Mountains on May 20, 1992. More recently, there is a third record with a photograph (currently uncatalogued) from El Paso, from December 5 to 14, 1995. Oberholser also refers to a historical specimen record dated September 12, 1916, from the Davis Mountains. There are many unsubmitted spring and fall reports, most from Big Bend National Park, by a variety of excellent observers. None, however, contains thorough documentation. *Review Species.*

Western Wood-Pewee *(Contopus sordidulus)*

Common migrant throughout and a common, though somewhat local, breeding species. Nesting occurs in the Guadalupe and Davis mountains as well as a few smaller mountain ranges in the northern Big Bend country. Although there are several summer reports from the Chisos Mountains and El Paso County, there is no evidence of breeding in either area. Migrants lingering well into June or early nesters returning in late July probably account for most of these sightings.

Eastern Wood-Pewee *(Contopus virens)*

Uncommon breeding bird along wooded streams in the southeastern Trans-Pecos. Eastern Wood-Pewees are considered casual throughout the entire region during migration, but identification problems with the Western Wood-Pewee cloud its status. Oberholser refers to one spring specimen taken in Brewster County (unknown location).

Yellow-bellied Flycatcher *(Empidonax flaviventris)*

Accidental. There are one record of a bird banded and photographed from the Davis Mountains (September 1, 1994) and two records of collected specimens from Big Bend National Park (September 3, 1968, and September 1, 1969).

Acadian Flycatcher *(Empidonax virescens)*

Rare and local summer resident in Val Verde County—the western edge of its North American breeding range. Its distribution in the eastern Trans-Pecos is thin and confined to small pockets of riparian woodland. Most observations are from the Devils River area.

Willow Flycatcher *(Empidonax traillii)*

Fairly common to uncommon migrant. Somewhat more numerous in the fall when migrants arrive as early as mid-July. Casual in summer in the western half of the Trans-Pecos, but no confirmed breeding since 1890. Oberholser's reference to this 1890 Brewster County nest record is "15 miles northwest of Alpine" (which actually would be in Jeff Davis County). The subspecies of Willow Flycatcher which breeds in the southwestern United States, and to which the 1890 breeding record refers, was listed as an endangered subspecies in February 1995. Details are appreciated for any nesting *empidonax* flycatcher in the Trans-Pecos, other than the Cordilleran Flycatcher.

Least Flycatcher *(Empidonax minimus)*

Fairly common spring and fall migrant in the eastern counties of the Trans-Pecos. Decidedly less numerous as one moves west through the region. A rare to casual migrant in the western counties, with most sightings from the fall.

Hammond's Flycatcher *(Empidonax hammondii)*

Uncommon migrant except in the southeastern Trans-Pecos, where it is generally absent. There are two published winter records, one observation from McKittrick Canyon in the Guadalupe Mountains and one from El Paso County.

Dusky Flycatcher *(Empidonax oberholseri)*

Fairly common to uncommon migrant except in the eastern counties, where it is rare or absent altogether. Recent summer sightings around Dog Canyon in the Guadalupe Mountains may suggest breeding. Very uncommon and sporadic in winter in Big Bend country, mostly along the Rio Grande. Winter specimens have been obtained from both Brewster and Presidio counties.

Gray Flycatcher *(Empidonax wrightii)*

Uncommon to rare migrant through the central and western Trans-Pecos. A highly localized breeding bird in the Davis Mountains around Mt. Livermore. In 1991, a nest with four young was discovered and photographed on private property in the upper Madera Canyon of the Davis Mountains (TPRF #912), documenting the first nest record for Texas. This species was found in numbers from about 5,800 to 7,200 ft. in this vicinity and was tape recorded on several occasions (TBSL #207-14,18,19,20 and 208-03,20,25). The closest U.S. nesting population to the Mt. Livermore birds is in south-central New Mexico. There have been summer sightings in the Guadalupe Mountains, but there is no nesting evidence yet from that mountain range. Fall migrants, which arrive as early as late July, may account for some of the midsummer sightings. Very uncommon to rare in winter in Big Bend country, with numbers fluctuating from year to year.

Cordilleran Flycatcher *(Empidonax occidentalis)*

Uncommon to fairly common migrant in the central mountains of the Trans-Pecos and in the El Paso area. Uncommon summer resident in montane forests above 6,000 ft. This species prefers wooded canyons near permanent springs or seeps, generally placing its nest in a low bank along a mountain stream. A Western-type Flycatcher was photographed and heard calling at Rio Grande Village in Big Bend National Park on November 10, 1991. The bird created widespread debate, with some observers believing that it may have been a Pacific-slope Flycatcher and not a Cordilleran. The status of Pacific-slope Flycatcher in the Trans-Pecos will remain unclear until more thorough documentation is obtained.

Black Phoebe *(Sayornis nigricans)*

Fairly common to uncommon breeding bird throughout most of the Trans-Pecos. Populations decline in some areas in winter (mostly at higher elevations) while increasing in others (such as El

Paso and Hudspeth counties). Their migration appears to vary both in altitude and latitude. Black Phoebes are nearly always found near water and may frequent lakes, ponds, and streams, as well as larger rivers like the Rio Grande.

Eastern Phoebe *(Sayornis phoebe)*

Uncommon migrant through the eastern two-thirds of the region and rare in the western third. Uncommon wintering bird west to Big Bend country. Casual in the far western counties in midwinter. Rare and local nesting bird in Val Verde and Terrell counties along some of the stream systems.

Say's Phoebe *(Sayornis saya)*

Fairly common breeding bird. Common in winter and in migration. Often associated with man-made structures that are utilized for nest sites. Say's Phoebes have been known to nest as early as February.

Vermilion Flycatcher *(Pyrocephalus rubinus)*

A common to fairly common breeding bird through much of the region, generally in close association with water. The exception to this status is the northern part of Hudspeth County and all of El Paso County, where this species is considered rare and does not breed. Uncommon in winter, with more northerly populations migrating out of the area altogether. Winter birds in the southern Trans-Pecos are most likely encountered along the Rio Grande.

Dusky-capped Flycatcher *(Myiarchus tuberculifer)*

Casual visitor to the Trans-Pecos, with most records from May and June. Most reviewed sightings are from the Chisos and Davis mountains. Probably a very rare nester in the Davis Mountains, where one pair was observed behaving in a territorial manner near the top of Mt. Livermore in June 1991. These Mt. Livermore birds were documented with tape recordings (TBSL #208-02) and photographs (TPRF #1020). In an effort to evaluate the birds at this location, a census was conducted the following summer. During that census, six pairs of Dusky-capped Flycatchers were discovered in the same general area. Unfortunately, follow-up surveys to confirm nesting were not possible. Overall, there are very few reviewed records for Texas. Specimens exist for El Paso and Brewster counties, and there are unsubmitted sightings elsewhere in the region. *Review Species.*

Ash-throated Flycatcher *(Myiarchus cinerascens)*

Common in spring and summer. Breeds in a wide variety of habitats from desert shrub to riparian thickets to oak-juniper woodlands above 5,000 ft. Breeding birds disperse quickly after nesting, often becoming hard to find by mid-August. Very uncommon in fall and rare and sporadic in winter, with most winter records from Big Bend country.

Great Crested Flycatcher *(Myiarchus crinitus)*

Casual to very rare migrant, with observations from late August through October. Sightings are from scattered counties, with the greatest concentration of records in Brewster County (including three specimen records from Big Bend National Park) and El Paso County. This species does breed, however, east of the Pecos River in Val Verde County, where it is considered a rare and local summer resident.

Brown-crested Flycatcher *(Myiarchus tyrannulus)*

Fairly common summer resident in Val Verde County and perhaps nesting along Independence Creek in Terrell County. A casual breeding bird west to Big Bend National Park (where it may be increasing) and north to El Paso County.

Great Kiskadee *(Pitangus sulphuratus)*

Uncommon but regular in Val Verde County. Casual in winter. Accidental west of the Pecos River, with four reports from Big Bend country. There are no records or sightings of any kind in the northern Trans-Pecos.

Sulphur-bellied Flycatcher *(Myiodynastes luteiventris)*

Accidental. There is one accepted record with a photograph from Pine Springs in the Chisos Mountains (July 28–August 8, 1997). Wauer lists five unsubmitted sightings between 1969 and 1991— most between April and August and all of them from Big Bend National Park. This largely tropical flycatcher has made several documented trips to Texas, but most of the reviewed sightings have been from south Texas.

1. Guadalupe Mountains, El Capitan peak, Culberson Co. (photo by Greg Lasley)

2. Davis Mountains, ca. 5,200 ft., Jeff Davis Co. (photo by Greg Lasley)

3. Davis Mountains, ca. 6,200 ft., Jeff Davis Co. (photo by Greg Lasley)

4. Ft. Hancock Reservoir, Hudspeth Co. (photo by Greg Lasley)

5. *Franklin Mountains State Park, El Paso Co. (photo by Barry Zimmer)*

6. *Ft. Bliss Sewage Ponds, El Paso Co. (photo by Barry Zimmer)*

7. Common Black-Hawk
(photo by Barry Zimmer)

8. Zone-tailed Hawk
(photo by Barry Zimmer)

9. Chisos Mountains, Big
Bend National Park,
Brewster Co. (photo by
Barry Zimmer)

10. Western and Clark's grebes (photo by Barry Zimmer)

11. Rain on the Rio Grande, Big Bend National Park, Brewster Co. (photo by Barry Zimmer)

12. *Ferruginous Hawk (photo by Barry Zimmer)*

13. *Montezuma Quail (photo by Barry Zimmer)*

14. Scaled Quail (photo by Barry Zimmer)

15. Gambel's Quail (photo by Barry Zimmer)

(opposite top)
*16. Mountain Plover
(photo by Barry Zimmer)*

(opposite bottom)
*17. Western Screech-Owl
(photo by Greg Lasley)*

(left)
*18. Elf Owl (photo by
Barry Zimmer)*

(below)
*19. Burrowing Owl (photo
by Barry Zimmer)*

(above)
*20. Scissor-tailed Flycatcher
(photo by Barry Zimmer)*

(right)
*21. Cordilleran Flycatcher
(photo by Greg Lasley)*

(opposite top)
*22. Violet-green Swallow
(photo by Barry Zimmer)*

(opposite bottom)
*23. Cave Swallow (photo by
Barry Zimmer)*

24. *Cactus Wren (photo by Barry Zimmer)*

25. *Phainopepla (photo by Barry Zimmer)*

26. *Western Bluebird (photo by Greg Lasley)*

27. *Gray Vireo (photo by Barry Zimmer)*

28. Colima Warbler (photo by Bob and Vera Thornton)

29. Grace's Warbler (photo by Barry Zimmer)

30. *Townsend's Warbler (photo by Barry Zimmer)*

31. *Painted Bunting (photo by Barry Zimmer)*

32. Black-throated Sparrow (photo by Barry Zimmer)

33. Green-tailed Towhee (photo by Barry Zimmer)

Tropical Kingbird *(Tyrannus melancholicus)*

There is one record at Cottonwood Campground in Big Bend National Park (June 24–August 3, 1996) of a nesting pair of Tropical Kingbirds. The nest was blown down in a windstorm, and no young were ever observed. This series of observations contains good written details and a tape recording. No definitive field marks exist for visually separating Tropical from Couch's kingbirds in the field, and any accepted record of this species will likely have to be accompanied by recordings. *Review Species.*

Couch's Kingbird *(Tyrannus couchii)*

Uncommon but regular in much of Val Verde County during spring, summer, and fall. Otherwise a casual visitor to Big Bend National Park, where scattered sight records are thought to be this species. A definitive specimen was taken from the park on September 2, 1968. Calls and song are diagnostic, but Couch's Kingbird cannot be safely distinguished from Tropical Kingbird on visual field marks alone.

Cassin's Kingbird *(Tyrannus vociferans)*

Common to fairly common breeding bird from the Guadalupe Mountains south through the Davis Mountains and into northern Brewster and Presidio counties. It does not nest, however, along the Rio Grande drainage. This species is an uncommon migrant throughout the region and can be found in a variety of habitats. In general, Cassin's Kingbirds prefer higher elevations and more wooded areas than the similar Western Kingbird. Casual in winter, with three sightings from Brewster and Jeff Davis counties.

Thick-billed Kingbird *(Tyrannus crassirostris)*

Rare and irregular summer resident in the lower Big Bend country. Most often found in mature cottonwood galleries along the Rio Grande. This species was first documented for the state on June 21, 1967, in the Chisos Mountains. A handful of sightings followed in the 1970's and early 1980's. Beginning in 1988, a pair of Thick-billed Kingbirds successfully nested in Cottonwood Campground of Big Bend National Park, and it is believed the same birds continued nesting at this location through 1991. Numerous photos and tape recordings of these nest records exist. Casual in winter. There are no documented sightings in the Trans-Pecos outside of Big Bend country. *Review Species.*

Western Kingbird *(Tyrannus verticalis)*

Generally, a common migrant and summer resident in many areas of the Trans-Pecos, but the status of this species varies widely. It is an abundant summer resident in El Paso County, but an uncommon to rare summer resident in most of the lower Big Bend country. It is considered common to fairly common around Lake Balmorhea and uncommon in the Guadalupe Mountains. The most appropriate general statement that can be made regarding this bird in the Trans-Pecos is that Cassin's Kingbirds usually replace them at elevations above 4,500 ft.

Eastern Kingbird *(Tyrannus tyrannus)*

Very rare to casual migrant through much of the Trans-Pecos except in the far eastern portion of the region, where it is considered uncommon. Spring records are from May and June, while fall records are from late July through September. There is one winter report from Big Bend National Park, but without details.

Scissor-tailed Flycatcher *(Tyrannus forficatus)*

Fairly common to uncommon summer resident in the eastern Trans-Pecos and central grasslands. More numerous in Val Verde and Terrell counties. Generally an uncommon migrant in the lower Big Bend country. Breeds irregularly west to Alpine and historically as far west as El Paso, where the species is now only a casual migrant.

Rose-throated Becard *(Pachyramphus aglaiae)*

Accidental. One specimen record from Musquiz Canyon in the Davis Mountains (Dallas Museum of Natural History, July 18, 1973). There are several undocumented reports from Big Bend National Park. *Review Species.*

SHRIKES: Family Laniidae

Northern Shrike *(Lanius excubitor)*

Accidental in winter. Two records from El Paso County. One adult was observed November 25, 1977, at Hueco Tanks State Park, and an immature bird was seen on the west side of the city of El Paso on December 9, 1978. There is a third record with details from Guadalupe Mountains National Park during a Christmas Count (December 1988).

Loggerhead Shrike *(Lanius ludovicianus)*

Common winter resident and fairly common to uncommon breeding bird. This species seems to prefer yucca-grassland associations to mesquite-creosote habitat for breeding purposes.

VIREOS: Family Vireonidae

White-eyed Vireo *(Vireo griseus)*

Rare spring migrant and winter visitor in the southern Trans-Pecos. Most records are from Val Verde, Terrell, and Brewster counties. Recent observations of singing birds from Independence Creek in Terrell County may suggest nesting.

Bell's Vireo *(Vireo bellii)*

Locally common summer resident (March through September) along the Rio Grande and along smaller washes in Big Bend country. Uncommon to rare in the northern and eastern Trans-Pecos, where habitat loss and cowbird parasitism have had a significant impact.

Black-capped Vireo *(Vireo atricapillus)*

Rare summer resident in the southern Trans-Pecos. Breeding populations are localized. Established populations of Black-capped Vireos exist along Independence Creek in Terrell County, along the Devils River in Val Verde County, and eastward into the Edwards Plateau. There is only scattered nesting west into Brewster and Presidio counties (although it is a rare, regular nester in the Chisos Mountains). This endangered species becomes increasingly rare to the north, with only one sighting from Jeff Davis County and no records at all for El Paso and Hudspeth counties.

Gray Vireo *(Vireo vicinior)*

Rare to uncommon summer resident. Very rare in winter. This bird generally prefers ravines and hillsides for nesting habitat. As is the case with the Black-capped Vireo, however, there is a significant amount of appropriate habitat where there are no birds. Nesting occurs in some of the lower canyons of the Guadalupe, Davis, and Chisos mountains as well as some smaller, scattered hills and washes. Accidental in El Paso County. The Gray Vireo is sometimes confused with the Plumbeous Vireo, but because of the Gray Vireo's much thinner eye-ring and complete lack of spectacles it should be relatively easy to identify.

Blue-headed Vireo *(Vireo solitarius)*

Rare migrant and casual wintering bird in the Trans-Pecos, with far fewer reports than the following two species. Recently split from Solitary Vireo (*Vireo solitarius*) into three distinct species: Blue-headed, Cassin's, and Plumbeous vireo. Blue-headed Vireos are the most brightly colored of the three species and show yellow flanks, gray heads, and olive-green backs.

Cassin's Vireo *(Vireo cassinii)*

Uncommon migrant in the Trans-Pecos. Very rare in winter. Records indicate more observations from fall than spring. Cassin's Vireos show more olive green around head and face and have paler yellow flanks than the Blue-headed Vireo. Recently split from Solitary Vireo.

Plumbeous Vireo *(Vireo plumbeus)*

Fairly common migrant and rare winter visitor throughout the Trans-Pecos. Common summer resident in the northern mountain ranges, particularly at elevations above 5,500 ft. *Vireo solitarius*, previously known as Solitary Vireo, was split into Blue-headed, Cassin's, and Plumbeous vireo. Overall, the Plumbeous Vireo has almost no yellow-olive tones in the upper parts or flanks (generally all gray) and no distinguishable contrast between the head and back. Misidentification of the Plumbeous Vireo is most likely to occur in fall when it sometimes shows a twinge of olive tones in the flanks, giving the impression of a dull or immature Cassin's Vireo.

Yellow-throated Vireo *(Vireo flavifrons)*

Uncommon to casual migrant. Possibly a local nester along Independence Creek in Terrell County and an uncommon but estab-

Black-capped Vireo

lished nester east of the Pecos River in southern Val Verde County. There are two June records from the Guadalupe Mountains, but nesting is not suspected in that mountain range.

Hutton's Vireo *(Vireo huttoni)*

Fairly common summer resident and uncommon winter resident in the Chisos and Davis mountains. There is one summer record from the Guadalupe Mountains National Park (1988), but there is no nesting evidence from that mountain range as of yet. Rare elsewhere in the Trans-Pecos, particularly at low elevations. Nests almost exclusively above 5,500 ft.

Warbling Vireo *(Vireo gilvus)*

Common to fairly common migrant. Common summer resident high in the Guadalupe Mountains and generally a rare nester in the Davis and Chisos mountains. DNA evidence suggests the possibility of at least two distinct species. If accepted as different species by the A.O.U., they would likely assume the common names of Eastern and Western Warbling vireos. The Western Warbling Vireo is apparently the nesting bird of the Trans-Pecos, but there is little information on visually separating these two supposedly distinct birds in the field. There are vocalization differences, but, if the split occurs, there are no records available to indicate whether the would-be eastern species has been observed in the Trans-Pecos.

Philadelphia Vireo *(Vireo philadelphicus)*

Casual spring and very rare fall migrant in the Trans-Pecos. Most fall records are August–September.

Red-eyed Vireo *(Vireo olivaceus)*

Very rare migrant in most of the Trans-Pecos. However, this species appears to be an uncommon nester east of the Pecos River in southern Val Verde County.

Yellow-green Vireo *(Vireo flavoviridus)*

Accidental. One specimen record from Cottonwood Campground in Big Bend National Park on July 13, 1972 (specimen at Northwest Missouri State University #DAE 2686) and a second report from that park of a singing male (May 7–8, 1980). *Review Species.*

JAYS AND CROWS: Family Corvidae

Steller's Jay *(Cyanocitta stelleri)*

Common resident in the high coniferous forests of the Guadalupe Mountains. An uncommon resident in higher elevations of the Davis Mountains, but absent as a breeder in the Chisos Mountains of Big Bend National Park. Sporadic and irregular in fall, winter, and spring throughout much of the central and western portions of the region during invasion years. Invasions occur on the average about once every five years as birds move down out of the mountains in search of food. These movements usually coincide with similar lowland invasions of other corvid species such as the Western Scrub-Jay and Pinyon Jay.

Blue Jay *(Cyanocitta cristata)*

Casual fall and winter visitor. This species has been known to invade the Trans-Pecos during certain years. The closest resident population occurs in the eastern Edwards Plateau.

Green Jay *(Cyanocorax yncas)*

Very rare and irregular in winter near Del Rio (Val Verde County), where a few birds have been observed on recent Christmas Bird Counts. Absent elsewhere in the Trans-Pecos.

Western Scrub-Jay *(Aphelocoma californica)*

Common permanent resident in the Davis and Guadalupe mountains as well as a few smaller ranges in northern Presidio and Brewster counties where suitable oak-juniper habitat exists. Uncommon resident in appropriate habitat in eastern portions of the region such as Terrell and Pecos counties. It is a rare and possibly irregular nester in the Chisos Mountains above 4,500 ft. (the Mexican Jay is the most commonly observed jay in the Chisos Mountains). Irregular fall, winter, and spring visitor to lowlands in the El Paso area, where it is common some years and absent others.

Mexican Jay *(Aphelocoma ultramarina)*

Common permanent resident only in the high country of the Chisos Mountains in Big Bend National Park. Despite numerous reports from other areas of the Trans-Pecos, this sedentary species has been documented only once outside the park. This record was a specimen taken 5 miles south of Alpine, Texas, in northern Brewster County on March 25, 1935. Previously referred to as Gray-breasted Jay.

Pinyon Jay *(Gymnorhinus cyanocephalus)*

Uncommon to very rare and very irregular winter visitor. Some years large flocks have been known to invade the Davis and Guadalupe mountains, occasionally reaching the El Paso area. Accidental elsewhere, with sightings from Brewster, Reeves, and Val Verde counties. This species is very unpredictable and can be noticeably absent for several years before recurring.

Clark's Nutcracker *(Nucifraga columbiana)*

Casual and highly irregular in fall, winter, and spring. Six documented records between 1969 and 1973, including five specimens. An unprecedented invasion occurred in the fall and winter of 1972 when nutcrackers were seen in numbers in at least four counties in the Trans-Pecos. Since that time, documented records exist only from the Guadalupe Mountains (three birds on November 27, 1987) and from Big Bend National Park (January 1, 1993). There are other scattered sightings which contain no documentation or have not been submitted for review. *Review Species.*

Black-billed Magpie *(Pica pica)*

Accidental. There is one accepted record for the Trans-Pecos (El Paso County, TPRF #890, February 4–17, 1990). There are six other sightings unsubmitted for review. All seven reports are relegated to Brewster, Jeff Davis, and El Paso counties. *Review Species.*

American Crow *(Corvus brachyrhynchos)*

Locally common to uncommon in winter in agricultural areas along the Rio Grande in El Paso and Hudspeth counties. In these two counties, this species has been known to invade area pecan groves in flocks numbering over a thousand. Casual around Del Rio in Val Verde County and perhaps accidental elsewhere. Scattered sightings exist in many areas of the Trans-Pecos, but the majority of them are undocumented. The frequent misidentification of this species with the Chihuahuan Raven makes most observations suspect.

Chihuahuan Raven *(Corvus cryptoleucus)*

Fairly common summer resident in desert shrub, grasslands, and mesquite flats throughout most of the region. Rare in lower Big Bend country. It is less common, or at least less widespread, in winter. In El Paso County, however, numbers actually increase in winter, with large flocks of birds inhabiting agricultural areas and local dumps. Generally replaced by Common Ravens in foothills, canyons, and higher mountains.

Common Raven *(Corvus corax)*

Common to uncommon permanent resident in the mountains and high canyons of the Trans-Pecos. This species may frequent lower areas in winter, but it generally stays in proximity to the mountains. The vast majority of ravens along the Rio Grande in Big Bend National Park and in the vicinity of the Chisos, Davis, and Guadalupe mountains are Common Ravens. Oddly, this species is largely absent from El Paso and Hudspeth counties.

LARKS: Family Alaudidae

Horned Lark *(Eremophila alpestris)*

A common to fairly common resident of grasslands throughout the Trans-Pecos. Generally absent as a breeding bird in dry regions such as Big Bend country and El Paso County. More widespread in winter when flocks often move into agricultural areas and drier deserts.

SWALLOWS: Family Hirundinidae

Purple Martin *(Progne subis)*

Uncommon spring and summer resident (mid-February–July) in the vicinity of Del Rio in Val Verde County. Very rare migrant throughout the remainder of the Trans-Pecos with the exception of the El Paso area, where it is considered casual. Specimen records exist for Big Bend National Park and the Davis Mountains.

Tree Swallow *(Tachycineta bicolor)*

Fairly common to uncommon migrant throughout the region. Spring migrants may appear as early as mid-February. Rare in winter along the Rio Grande in the southeastern portion of the Trans-Pecos. Casual in that season north and west along the river to Big Bend National Park and El Paso.

Violet-green Swallow *(Tachycineta thalassina)*

Fairly common to uncommon summer resident in the higher portions of the Chisos, Davis, Franklin, and Guadalupe mountains. Fairly common migrant through the central and western parts of the region. Rare to casual in the easternmost portion of the Trans-Pecos. As with the Tree Swallow, northbound migrants appear as early as mid-February. Accidental in winter, with reports from Big Bend National Park and Del Rio.

Northern Rough-winged Swallow *(Stelgidopteryx serripennis)*

Fairly common to uncommon summer resident along major river systems throughout the Trans-Pecos. A fairly common migrant elsewhere within the region, often arriving in early February and sometimes lingering in fall until November. Uncommon to rare in winter along the Rio Grande from Big Bend country south and east. Accidental in winter north to El Paso and Hudspeth counties.

Bank Swallow *(Riparia riparia)*

Fairly common to uncommon migrant throughout the region. Generally arrives later in spring (late March) than other swallows. A casual, localized breeding bird currently known from one location only—a gravel pit near Del Rio where a colony of birds has nested for a number of years since at least 1989. May nest at other locations, but no other Trans-Pecos colonies are known at present. Nesting occurred in El Paso County in the 1940's, but there have been no nest records in recent times. Accidental in winter, with only one documented Trans-Pecos record from Big Bend National Park on December 8, 1967.

Barn Swallow *(Hirundo rustica)*

Abundant to common summer resident and migrant throughout the Trans-Pecos. Breeding birds generally choose man-made structures, such as buildings and bridges, for nest sites. Stragglers may be seen into late November or even early December, especially along the Rio Grande.

Cliff Swallow *(Petrocheldion pyrrhonota)*

Common to fairly common summer resident and migrant throughout most of the Trans-Pecos. Utilizes cliffs near water as well as a variety of man-made structures for nesting purposes. Because this species arrives later in spring than the Cave Swallow, it is finding that the availability of nesting habitat is being reduced—taken over by the Cave Swallow's blossoming range expansion.

Cave Swallow *(Petrocheldian fulva)*

Common to uncommon migrant throughout the region. Common to fairly common summer resident except in Big Bend country north to Jeff Davis County, where it is generally absent. Historically,

Cave Swallows nested only in limestone caves in the Edwards Plateau of Texas and at Carlsbad Caverns, New Mexico. In the last 15–20 years, however, this species has undergone a remarkable breeding range expansion. By utilizing highway overpasses, bridges, and culverts in much the same manner as Barn and Cliff swallows, they have spread rapidly across west Texas. Though never recorded in El Paso and Hudspeth counties until 1983, they are now more numerous than the Cliff Swallow in that area. Cave Swallows arrive in mass by late February, when many other swallows are just beginning their migration. In fall, large postbreeding congregations may appear, particularly in the areas around some of the larger lakes and reservoirs.

TITMICE AND CHICKADEES: Family Paridae

Carolina Chickadee *(Poecile carolinensis)*

Casual winter visitor around Del Rio in Val Verde County. The nearest nesting population occurs in Edwards County just east of the Trans-Pecos.

Black-capped Chickadee *(Poecile atricapillus)*

Accidental. There is one specimen record, recently uncovered by D. Sibley at Yale's Peabody Museum, dated April 10, 1881, from El Paso County (YPM #9723). Interestingly, Oberholser's only reference to the Black-capped Chickadee in Texas is to four specimens that were taken between 1880 and 1883, which may suggest a prolonged invasion in the early part of that decade. However, because these four specimens referred to by Oberholser have not yet been relocated, the Black-capped Chickadee's status has remained suspect in Texas. This newest Black-capped Chickadee record has been accepted by the TBRC and confirms the status of this species as a Texas bird. *Review Species.*

Mountain Chickadee *(Poecile gambeli)*

Common to fairly common permanent resident in higher elevations of the Davis and Guadalupe mountains. Absent from the Chisos Mountains. Irregular in fall and winter at lower elevations in the western third of the region.

Juniper Titmouse *(Baeolophus ridgwayi)*

Uncommon permanent resident in the oak-juniper foothills of the Guadalupe Mountains. Accidental winter visitor in the El Paso area. No documented records exist south of Culberson County. Formerly part of the Plain Titmouse complex.

Tufted Titmouse *(Baeolophus bicolor)*

Common permanent resident in oak-juniper woodlands in the central, southern, and eastern portions of the Trans-Pecos. Rare and localized resident at Lake Balmorhea and other low-elevation locations away from the mountains. Casual in the Guadalupe Mountains and elsewhere in the northern Trans-Pecos. It is possible this species may again be split into Black-crested Titmouse (*B. bicolor dysleptus* in the Trans-Pecos) and Tufted Titmouse (*B. b. bicolor*). The Black-crested Titmouse is the resident form in the Trans-Pecos, with no known records of *B. b. bicolor*.

PENDULANT TITS: Family Remizidae

Verdin *(Auriparus flaviceps)*

Common to uncommon permanent resident in a variety of low-elevation habitats throughout the Trans-Pecos. Generally found in desert shrub, mesquite flats, and brushy arroyos, as well as salt cedar thickets and open riparian edge.

BUSHTITS: Family Aegithalidae

Bushtit *(Psaltriparus minimus)*

Common permanent resident in oak-juniper woodlands throughout the region. Less common in pine woodlands above 7,500 ft. Casual in fall and winter at lower elevations. The Bushtit is a highly gregarious species that is most often encountered in small flocks. Juvenile males in the Southwest have a distinct ear patch and were once considered a separate species known as the Black-eared Bushtit.

NUTHATCHES: Family Sittidae

Red-breasted Nuthatch *(Sitta canadensis)*

Irregular fall, winter, and spring visitor throughout the Trans-Pecos. There are summer records from the Guadalupe Mountains and at least one breeding record of a nest with young from that mountain range (photograph, TPRF #1047, May 31, 1993). This species is entirely invasionary in winter, being rather common during some years and completely absent in others. May be encountered in a variety of wooded habitats, including mountains, foothills, riparian woodlands, and even residential neighborhoods.

White-breasted Nuthatch *(Sitta carolinensis)*

Common to fairly common permanent resident in high-elevation forests, usually above 5,000 ft. Rare to casual fall and winter visitor elsewhere in the Trans-Pecos. Generally absent from the eastern portion of the region. This species is encountered far less frequently than the highly irruptive Red-breasted Nuthatch.

Pygmy Nuthatch *(Sitta pygmaea)*

Fairly common to uncommon resident in the high-elevation forests of the Guadalupe Mountains above 7,000 ft. Rare permanent resident in the highest parts of the Davis Mountains. A casual fall and winter visitor in the Chisos Mountains and in the El Paso area during invasion years.

CREEPERS: Family Certhidae

Brown Creeper *(Certhia americana)*

Uncommon to rare fall migrant and winter resident throughout the region. Though most often encountered in the mountains, this species also occurs irregularly in riparian areas at low elevations. It is a rare breeding bird in the Guadalupe Mountains and perhaps the Davis Mountains, where summer sightings have occurred.

WRENS: Family Troglodytidae

Cactus Wren *(Campylorhynchus brunneicapillus)*

Common permanent resident throughout the Trans-Pecos. Found in a variety of habitats, from desert flats to lower oak-juniper woodlands up to 6,000 ft. The Cactus Wren is a noisy and conspicuous species that is easily seen in most regions.

Rock Wren *(Salpinctes obsoletus)*

Common to fairly common permanent resident throughout the Trans-Pecos. Occurs in a variety of rocky habitats, from arroyos and rocky foothills to higher mountain canyons. Prefers more open areas and avoids heavily forested slopes. Some individuals migrate to lower elevations in winter.

Canyon Wren *(Catherpes mexicanus)*

Common to fairly common permanent resident in rocky, mountainous terrain and low-elevation canyons throughout the region. Heard more often than seen, the Canyon Wren's falling-note song may be the most memorable of any North American songbird.

Carolina Wren *(Thryothorus ludovicianus)*

Uncommon resident in riparian areas in Val Verde County and eastern portions of Terrell County. Rare to casual visitor in all seasons in the remainder of the Trans-Pecos, with records from as far west as Hudspeth and El Paso counties. In the last several years, at least one territorial pair has been present in the vicinity of the nature trail at Rio Grande Village in Big Bend National Park and is presumed to be nesting.

Bewick's Wren *(Thryomanes bewickii)*

Common to fairly common permanent resident in oak-juniper woodlands throughout the region. A localized nester in other habitats and at lower elevations. Fairly common migrant and winter resident through the remainder of the Trans-Pecos, often in desert shrub, brushy arroyos, and riparian areas.

House Wren *(Troglodytes aedon)*

Fairly common migrant and uncommon winter resident throughout most of the Trans-Pecos. Uncommon and local breeding bird in the upper elevations of the Guadalupe and Davis mountains. Winter numbers fluctuate from year to year, with more individuals present in milder winters.

Winter Wren *(Troglodytes troglodytes)*

Rare to casual migrant and winter visitor throughout the Trans-Pecos. Most records are from November, coinciding with peak fall movements. Usually found in moist thickets and dense tangles in riparian habitats. Shy and somewhat secretive on its wintering grounds.

Sedge Wren *(Cistothorus platensis)*

A very rare, local migrant and winter resident. The majority of records are from Lake Balmorhea, where this species has been found with some regularity in wet, grassy areas near the dam. One photograph record from Hudspeth County (May 17, 1984).

Marsh Wren (*Cistothorus palustris*)

Common to fairly common migrant and winter resident in marshy habitats throughout the region. There is one historical nest record from El Paso County (April 10, 1938), but no recent evidence of nesting has been observed.

DIPPERS: Family Cinclidae

American Dipper *(Cinclus mexicanus)*

Casual in fall and winter. There are four accepted records and several additional reliable sightings from the Trans-Pecos. Two of the records are from the Guadalupe Mountains National Park, spanning the fall and winter seasons of 1987–1988 and 1988–1989. There are also documented records from El Paso (November 8–16, 1984) and from Big Bend National Park (March 12, 1986). Also reported from Brewster, Culberson, Jeff Davis, and Presidio counties. *Review Species.*

KINGLETS: Family Regulidae

Golden-crowned Kinglet *(Regulus satrapa)*

Very uncommon to rare migrant and winter visitor. Most often observed in high-elevation woodlands of the Guadalupe and Davis mountains, where it is seen during most, but not all, winters. It is rare and irregular in nearly all other areas of the Trans-Pecos.

Ruby-crowned Kinglet *(Regulus calendula)*

Abundant to common migrant throughout the Trans-Pecos. Common in winter through most of the region, but generally absent in higher elevations during that season.

GNATCATCHERS: Family Muscicapidae

Blue-gray Gnatcatcher *(Polioptila caerulea)*

Common to uncommon nester in oak-juniper woodlands of the Chisos, Guadalupe, and some of the smaller mountain ranges. The exception is the Davis Mountains, where its nesting status remains unclear. Nests locally in similar habitat east of Big Bend country. Fairly common to uncommon migrant through much of the Trans-Pecos. Less numerous in northwest portions of the region. In winter, Blue-gray Gnatcatchers are very uncommon and irregular. During this season, they are occasionally found in riparian areas at lower elevations from Hudspeth County south and east to Val Verde County.

Black-tailed Gnatcatcher *(Polioptila melanura)*

A fairly common permanent resident in lower Big Bend country east to the Devils River in Val Verde County. Very uncommon to rare local resident of desert shrub throughout the remainder of the Trans-Pecos.

THRUSHES: Subfamily Turdinae

Eastern Bluebird *(Sialia sialis)*

Uncommon to rare migrant and winter visitor. Somewhat irregular.

There is one nest record of birds with young from Rio Grande Village in Big Bend National Park during the spring of 1972 (R. H. Wauer).

Western Bluebird *(Sialia mexicana)*

Common to fairly common permanent resident in the Davis and Guadalupe mountains. A fairly common winter visitor to the Chisos Mountains, but not known to nest. This bird will occasionally visit lowland habitats in winter, particularly in El Paso and Hudspeth counties, where it can be fairly common at that time of year. It is more commonly seen in wooded foothills and mountains.

Mountain Bluebird *(Sialia currucoides)*

Fairly common to uncommon migrant and winter resident, but very irregular. This species congregates in flocks and can be locally common in some grassland areas, particularly around the foothills of the Davis and Guadalupe mountains. It is uncommon in the El Paso area and rare in the southeastern part of the Trans-Pecos. There is one 1995 record (July 31) of an adult attending juveniles in the Davis Mountains which is considered the first breeding record for the state.

Townsend's Solitaire *(Myadestes townsendi)*

Fairly common to uncommon migrant and winter resident. This species can be irregular, particularly at lower elevations. In most years, it is seen most commonly in the Guadalupe Mountains.

Veery *(Catharus fuscescens)*

Accidental migrant in the Trans-Pecos. Several observations from Big Bend National Park (R. H. Wauer).

Swainson's Thrush *(Catharus ustulatus)*

Casual migrant through most of the Trans-Pecos. Most records are from the major mountain ranges.

Hermit Thrush *(Catharus guttatus)*

Common to fairly common migrant and winter resident near mountains and foothills. Generally uncommon at lower elevations. Fairly common summer resident in the high forests of the Davis and Guadalupe mountains.

Wood Thrush *(Hylocichla mustelina)*

Casual in winter and in migration. Two El Paso records and a few sightings from Big Bend National Park.

Rufous-backed Robin *(Turdus rufopalliatus)*

Accidental. There are three records for the area. One record is from Val Verde County (photograph, TPRF #116, November 11–18, 1976), one is from the Davis Mountains (February 9, 1992), and one record was a bird found dead in El Paso (specimen at University of Texas–El Paso, October 27, 1993). *Review Species.*

American Robin *(Turdus migratorius)*

Fairly common migrant and winter resident. Locally common to uncommon breeding bird. This species is a common summer resident in the Guadalupe Mountains and an uncommon breeder in the Davis Mountains, and is generally absent in summer from the Chisos Mountains. It is a locally uncommon breeding bird in El Paso.

Varied Thrush *(Ixoreus naevius)*

Casual visitor to the Trans-Pecos. There are six accepted records and one historical sighting. Observations are from El Paso, the Guadalupe Mountains, Lake Balmorhea, the Davis Mountains, and Big Bend National Park. The seasonal range is from October 3 through May 10. *Review Species.*

Aztec Thrush *(Ridgwayia pinicola)*

Accidental. There are two documented records from Boot Spring in Big Bend National Park (TPRF #125, August 21–25, 1977, and July 31–August 7, 1982). *Review Species.*

MOCKINGBIRDS AND THRASHERS: Family Mimidae

Gray Catbird *(Dumetella carolinensis)*

Casual. Scattered sightings throughout the Trans-Pecos, with most observations in spring and fall.

Northern Mockingbird *(Mimus polyglottos)*

Abundant to common summer resident. Fairly common to uncommon in winter. Somewhat local in winter around El Paso, where birds are found largely in city suburbs, but not in the surrounding desert. Found in nearly every habitat but the high-elevation forests. Many of the birds migrate completely out of the area in spring and are replaced by birds that have wintered farther to the south.

Sage Thrasher *(Oreoscoptes montanus)*

Uncommon migrant and winter resident. Somewhat irregular. Most easily found around Guadalupe Mountains National Park. Numbers are highest when invading frugivores (e.g., bluebirds) are at their peak.

Brown Thrasher *(Toxostoma rufum)*

Rare migrant and winter resident. Although this eastern species seems far out of place in the Chihuahuan Desert, it generally shows up every year somewhere in the Trans-Pecos.

Long-billed Thrasher *(Toxostoma longirostre)*

Rare to casual wanderer in the southern half of the Trans-Pecos. Sightings are more likely in the southeastern Trans-Pecos, but there are several records for Big Bend National Park. There has been some nesting in Kinney County (1991) just east of Val Verde County.

Curve-billed Thrasher *(Toxostoma curvirostre)*

Common to uncommon migrant and winter resident. Somewhat localized breeding bird ranging from rare in the El Paso area to fairly common in Big Bend country to common in the Davis and Guadalupe mountains. In breeding season, it is more often observed in yucca-grassland assocations than mesquite-creosote habitats.

Crissal Thrasher *(Toxostoma crissale)*

Fairly common to uncommon permanent resident in dry desert shrub, mountain canyons, and salt cedar bosques along the Rio Grande. The center of abundance is in the northwestern Trans-Pecos. Because the Crissal Thrasher is shy and retiring, it may be more common than records indicate. It is perhaps more easily viewed from February to late April when birds are singing.

STARLINGS: Family Sturnidae

European Starling *(Sturnus vulgaris)*

Common permanent resident in cities and towns, but generally quite rare in uninhabited areas. Casual in Big Bend National Park.

PIPITS: Family Motacillidae

American Pipit *(Anthus rubescens)*

Common to fairly common migrant and winter resident. Often seen near water or in agricultural areas.

Sprague's Pipit *(Anthus spragueii)*

Casual migrant with some winter sightings. Most observations are from Big Bend country east to Val Verde County. Accidental in the northern Trans-Pecos.

WAXWINGS: Family Bombycillidae

Cedar Waxwing *(Bombycilla cedrorum)*

Locally fairly common winter bird (although somewhat irregular) and common to uncommon migrant. Juveniles have been seen at higher elevations in fall, but as yet there is no indication of nesting. This species is generally uncommon in Big Bend country.

SILKY FLYCATCHERS: Family Ptilogonatidae

Gray Silky-flycatcher *(Ptilogonys cinereus)*

Accidental. There is one accepted winter record of this bird for the Trans-Pecos, January 12–March 5, 1995, in El Paso County. This largely Mexican species has been seen only twice in the United States, both times in Texas. *Review Species.*

Phainopepla *(Phainopepla nitens)*

Generally an uncommon permanent resident and somewhat localized breeding bird. Although it is uncommon in the dry desert

Phainopepla

shrub, the status of this species changes to common in the foothills of the Davis Mountains, particularly around Davis Mountains State Park. It is very localized in the El Paso area, where it is found in wooded residential neighborhoods but not in the surrounding desert.

OLIVE WARBLERS: Family Peucedramidae

Olive Warbler *(Peucedramus taeniatus)*

Accidental. There are three accepted records for Texas, including one from Big Bend National Park (May 3, 1991), one from the Davis Mountains (TPRF #1094, May 19, 1992), and one from Big Bend Ranch (September 7, 1994). There are several unsubmitted reports from Big Bend country. This species nests just across the Rio

Grande within 50 miles of Big Bend National Park high in the Sierra Del Carmen Mountains of Mexico. *Review Species.*

WOOD WARBLERS: Family Parulidae

Blue-winged Warbler *(Vermivora pinus)*

Accidental. A few spring and late summer observations from Big Bend National Park (R. H. Wauer) by respected observers, but no details were ever submitted to *American Birds* magazine or other publications.

Golden-winged Warbler *(Vermivora chrysoptera)*

Casual in spring. All records are from Big Bend National Park and the El Paso area, and all dates are from early May. One hybrid "Brewster's" Warbler was observed April 28, 1996, in Big Bend National Park.

Tennessee Warbler *(Vermivora peregrina)*

Casual migrant throughout the Trans-Pecos. Spring dates are from April 30 to May 11, and fall dates are from September 19 to October 18. One winter record from Big Bend National Park.

Orange-crowned Warbler *(Vermivora celata)*

Fairly common migrant and uncommon winter resident. Fairly common nester in the high coniferous forests of the Guadalupe Mountains and a rare nester around the highest peaks of the Davis Mountains.

Nashville Warbler *(Vermivora ruficapilla)*

Rare to uncommon migrant throughout the Trans-Pecos.

Virginia's Warbler *(Vermivora virginiae)*

Fairly common to uncommon migrant. Fairly common nester in high coniferous forests of the Guadalupe Mountains and a rare, high-elevation nester in the Davis Mountains.

Colima Warbler *(Vermivora crissalis)*

Common to fairly common summer resident only in the high canyons of the Chisos Mountains. Colima Warblers are not known to nest anywhere else in the United States. This species frequents the oak woodlands and can usually be seen most easily near Boot Canyon in the spring and early summer.

Lucy's Warbler *(Vermivora luciae)*

Rare migrant and locally uncommon summer resident. Accidental in winter. This species nests locally along parts of the Rio Grande from Brewster County to Hudspeth County. A few birds have been nesting for the last several years at the Cottonwood Campground in Big Bend National Park, but the birds are not easily seen. It is uncommon to find this bird anywhere outside the Rio Grande floodplain.

Crescent-chested Warbler *(Parula superciliosa)*

Accidental. One record from Boot Canyon in Big Bend National Park (June 2, 1993). Since no photograph accompanied this record, Crescent-chested Warbler is currently accepted only on the "Presumptive List" of Texas birds. This species is generally found from Nicaragua to northern Mexico, but there are a handful of sightings from Arizona. *Review Species.*

Northern Parula *(Parula americana)*

Very rare migrant in the Trans-Pecos. Casual in winter, with records from Big Bend National Park and the Davis Mountains.

Tropical Parula *(Parula pitiayumi)*

Accidental. Two records from Big Bend National Park. The first record from the park is from Rio Grande Village and was reported from April 30 to May 1, 1994 (TPRF #1183). The second record from that area is of a bird observed April 26–27, 1996. Although Tropical Parula is not a review species, reports of this bird should be carefully documented, since the closely related Northern Parula has been seen in the Trans-Pecos with much more frequency.

Yellow Warbler *(Dendroica petechia)*

Fairly common migrant. Casual in winter. Yellow Warbler was formerly a nesting species from 3,500 to 5,000 ft. in the Trans-Pecos and a regular nesting bird in other parts of Texas. It is no longer known to nest anywhere in the state. Oberholser suggests climatic warming, destruction of streamside vegetation, and cowbird predation as contributing to the demise of Yellow Warbler as a Texas breeding bird.

Chestnut-sided Warbler *(Dendroica pensylvanica)*

Casual migrant. Records exist from Big Bend National Park and El Paso County. Spring records are from May 6 to 19, and fall records are from September 11 to November 23.

Magnolia Warbler *(Dendroica magnolia)*

Casual migrant. There have been at least ten reliable sightings. Spring observations from the month of May and all fall sightings from October and November.

Cape May Warbler *(Dendroica tigrina)*

Accidental in spring. Records are from Big Bend National Park (April 18–May 2, 1976, and May 3, 1988) and El Paso County (April 21–25, 1983). This species does not stray into the southwestern United States with the same frequency as many of the other eastern wood warblers.

Black-throated Blue Warbler *(Dendroica caerulescens)*

Casual migrant with most observations from the fall (the highest concentration is from late September to mid-October). This largely Caribbean species has wandered into the Trans-Pecos with some frequency in the 1990's. There is one specimen record from Big Bend National Park, which was collected June 22, 1971, and is currently a study skin (Northwest Missouri State University #DAE 2571) in the Big Bend National Park collection.

Yellow-rumped Warbler *(Dendroica coronata)*

The "Audubon's" form is a common migrant and winter resident and a fairly common summer resident above 7,000 ft. in both the Davis and Guadalupe mountains. The "Myrtle" form is an uncommon to rare migrant and winter resident throughout the Trans-Pecos.

Black-throated Gray Warbler *(Dendroica nigrascens)*

Uncommon to rare migrant. Casual winter visitor. One historical sighting of a downy juvenile in the Guadalupe Mountains, but nesting unconfirmed.

Townsend's Warbler *(Dendroica townsendi)*

Fairly common to uncommon migrant. Casual in winter.

Hermit Warbler *(Dendroica occidentalis)*

Rare migrant through most of the Trans-Pecos, with several records for the high country of the Chisos Mountains. Two winter records from Big Bend National Park.

Black-throated Green Warbler *(Dendroica virens)*

Casual migrant. Records are from Brewster and El Paso counties.

Golden-cheeked Warbler *(Dendroica chrysoparia)*

Casual. There are a total of four scattered reports from the Chisos Mountains in Big Bend National Park (R. H. Wauer). There are two observations from the month of April (1968 and 1978) and two from the month of July (1978 and 1980). This endangered species is rarely seen outside its nesting habitat in the hill country of central Texas.

Blackburnian Warbler *(Dendroica fusca)*

Casual spring migrant and accidental in fall. There are two fall records from El Paso, but most records and observations are from spring in Big Bend National Park.

Yellow-throated Warbler *(Dendroica dominica)*

Casual spring migrant. This species actually nests less than 100 miles east of Del Rio in Uvalde County. There are a few records for as far north as Guadalupe Mountains National Park.

Grace's Warbler *(Dendroica graciae)*

Common summer resident in coniferous or mixed woodlands above 5,500 ft. in the Davis and Guadalupe mountains. Rare migrant. Rainfall fluctuations appear to have some impact on local populations from year to year.

Pine Warbler *(Dendroica pinus)*

Casual. One record from the Guadalupe Mountains (November 20, 1991) and four records from Big Bend National Park, including a bird that apparently over-wintered two years in a row (1990–1991 and 1991–1992).

Prairie Warbler *(Dendroica discolor)*

Accidental. One record with photograph from Hudspeth County (November 19, 1987) and two records from Big Bend National Park (spring and summer, 1990).

Palm Warbler *(Dendroica palmarum)*

Casual migrant in the Trans-Pecos, with records from Brewster, El Paso, and Pecos counties. One winter record from El Paso County (December 14–17, 1993). Spring migration for this species may be as early as March and fall migration as late as mid-October.

Bay-breasted Warbler *(Dendroica castanea)*

One good written record from Santa Helena Canyon in Big Bend National Park on May 11, 1989. Very few published sightings from the Trans-Pecos.

Blackpoll Warbler *(Dendroica striata)*

Casual migrant throughout the Trans-Pecos. One winter record from El Paso (December 1993).

Black-and-White Warbler *(Mniotilta varia)*

Very uncommon to rare migrant. Casual in winter. More numerous in the eastern Trans-Pecos. Records exist for every month except February.

American Redstart *(Setophaga ruticilla)*

Very uncommon to rare migrant. There are a few summer reports and one winter record from El Paso (1993).

Prothonotary Warbler *(Protonotaria citrea)*

Casual migrant. One specimen record from El Paso County (May 7, 1974). There are at least four fall sightings from the northwest Trans-Pecos, ranging from late July to late September. One winter record from Big Bend National Park (February 23, 1991).

Worm-eating Warbler *(Helmitheros vermivorus)*

Very rare spring migrant. Two fall observations. Records from Brewster, Jeff Davis, Val Verde, and El Paso counties.

Swainson's Warbler *(Limnothlypis swainsonii)*

Accidental. One record of this species observed by a group of birders in Big Bend National Park (May 4, 1996). There is a second report of Swainson's Warbler from the Davis Mountains (April 27, 1996). The spring of 1996 brought several eastern warblers into the Trans-Pecos, but this humidity-loving species was perhaps the most unexpected.

Ovenbird *(Seiurus aurocapillus)*

Very rare migrant in the Trans-Pecos. Spring records are from late April through early June, and fall records are from mid-September to mid-October.

Northern Waterthrush *(Seiurus noveboracensis)*

Rare to uncommon migrant. Most records are from August through September.

Louisiana Waterthrush *(Seiurus motacilla)*

Casual migrant. In the Trans-Pecos, the Northern Waterthrush is much more likely to be seen than this species. There are three fall records from El Paso County and a few scattered sightings from as early as March from Brewster County.

Kentucky Warbler *(Oporornis formosus)*

Casual spring migrant. Records range from March 17 to May 11. Most sightings are from Brewster County.

Mourning Warbler *(Oporornis philadelphia)*

Accidental. One record of a bird caught in a mist net (Jeff Davis County, August 28–September 1, 1993), and one sighting from Big Bend National Park (April 18, 1972).

MacGillivray's Warbler *(Oporornis tolmiei)*

Fairly common migrant throughout the Trans-Pecos. A pair was seen behaving in a territorial manner in the Davis Mountains (1992), but nesting could not be confirmed.

Common Yellowthroat *(Geothlypis trichas)*

Fairly common migrant and summer resident, particularly along the Rio Grande floodplain. Uncommon to rare in winter.

Hooded Warbler *(Wilsonia citrina)*

Very rare migrant. Most observations are spring sightings ranging from April 18 to May 18. There are at least four fall sightings split between El Paso and Big Bend National Park that have a seasonal

Painted Redstart

range from September 1 to November 12. There is one summer sighting from the Chisos Mountains (June 16, 1979).

Wilson's Warbler *(Wilsonia pusilla)*

Abundant migrant throughout most of the Trans-Pecos. Casual in winter.

Canada Warbler *(Wilsonia canadensis)*

Accidental in migration. Scattered reports exist from around Big Bend National Park (R. H. Wauer).

Red-faced Warbler *(Cardellina rubrifrons)*

Casual migrant. There are nine records from the high country in the Chisos Mountains and three reviewed El Paso records. These records are scattered throughout the summer, with most records from August. Three records include photo documentation (TPRF #294, 277, and 1015). *Review Species.*

Painted Redstart *(Myioborus pictus)*

Rare and local summer resident. Casual in migration. This species nests only in the highest canyons of the Chisos and Davis mountains. One spring record from Guadalupe Mountains National Park. Populations apparently fluctuate. In some years it may be absent altogether.

Slate-throated Redstart *(Myioborus miniatus)*

Accidental. There are two accepted Trans-Pecos records of this largely tropical species. There is one accepted sight record from Boot Spring in the Chisos Mountains (April 30–May 15, 1990). Because this particular record contained only written documentation, the bird remained on the Texas "Presumptive List" for seven more years. The second record, from private property in the Davis Mountains (August 2, 1997), was well documented with both photographs and tape recordings (as yet uncatalogued). Slate-throated Redstart has now been moved to the official list of Texas birds. *Review Species.*

Rufous-capped Warbler *(Basileuterus rufifrons)*

Casual, usually in winter or spring. The seven total records in the Trans-Pecos include four from Big Bend National Park, one from Seminole Canyon State Park. Two of the Big Bend records include photos (TPRF #1065 and #165). There are two accepted records from Dolan Creek in Val Verde County (January 10–March 9, 1993, and August 30, 1995). Many of these birds stayed for long periods of time, with one bird in Big Bend reported continuously from September 9, 1973, through June 29, 1974. *Review Species.*

Yellow-breasted Chat *(Icteria virens)*

Common to uncommon summer resident, particularly along the Rio Grande floodplain. It can occasionally be found in seeps or moist areas as high as 5,000 ft. Less common as a migrant away from the river.

TANAGERS: Family Thraupidae

Hepatic Tanager *(Piranga flava)*

Fairly common to uncommon summer resident in the major

mountain ranges, usually in woodlands above 5,500 ft. Rarely seen in migration. One winter record.

Summer Tanager *(Piranga rubra)*

Common to uncommon migrant and summer resident. This species can be quite common in the cottonwoods around rivers and streams. It is usually replaced at higher elevations by the Hepatic Tanager.

Scarlet Tanager *(Piranga olivacea)*

Casual migrant. A few scattered records throughout the Trans-Pecos ranging from April to July.

Western Tanager *(Piranga ludoviciana)*

Fairly common migrant. Common to uncommon breeding bird in the Davis and Guadalupe mountains. Historical breeding bird in the Chisos Mountains, but no nest data recently. This bird can be seen just about anywhere in migration, but prefers high wooded canyons and coniferous forests for its nesting habitat. Most commonly seen as a summer resident in the canyons of Guadalupe Mountains National Park. Migrants appear at lowland locations by late July. One winter record (December 18, 1983) from El Paso.

Flame-colored Tanager *(Piranga bidentata)*

Accidental. Two spring records, both from the Chisos Mountains in mid-April of 1996. One bird was an adult male seen April 16–19 in Pine Canyon, and the other was an immature male seen around the Basin Campground on April 20–22. Both records have indentifiable photographs as yet uncatalogued. *Review Species.*

SPARROWS AND BUNTINGS: Family Emberizidae

Olive Sparrow *(Arremenops rufivirgatus)*

Rare and irregular visitor in southern Val Verde County only. No records west of the Pecos River.

Green-tailed Towhee *(Pipilo chlorurus)*

Fairly common migrant and winter resident except in Val Verde County, where it is rare. Rare summer resident in the Guadalupe and Davis mountains above 7,000 ft. There are summer sightings from the Chisos Mountains, but no evidence of nesting exists for that mountain range.

Eastern Towhee *(Pipilo erythrophthalmus)*

Accidental. The recent split of the Rufous-sided Towhee has yielded two physically distinct species—the Eastern Towhee and Spotted Towhee. Their range of overlap is fairly broad in Texas, but virtually all birds in the Trans-Pecos are Spotted Towhees. Although records may be limited because of its prior status, there is one record of the Eastern Towhee from El Paso County (March 4–22, 1987).

Spotted Towhee *(Pipilo maculatus)*

This now-distinct species is the result of a recent a.o.u. split of the Rufous-sided Towhee. The Spotted Towhee is a common to uncommon migrant and winter resident. It is a common to fairly common summer resident in the high forests of the Trans-Pecos.

Canyon Towhee *(Pipilo fuscus)*

Abundant to fairly common resident of the mountains and foothills. Some vertical migration in winter when birds may move into the lower desert.

Botteri's Sparrow *(Aimophila botterii)*

Accidental. One well-documented record of a mated pair (most likely the *arizonae* subspecies) from Presidio County, June 12, 1997, is the first known observation in Texas outside the Lower Rio Grande Valley. A juvenile later observed with the pair confirmed nesting. The *texana* subspecies found in south Texas has a small, local nesting range and rarely strays from a few coasal counties.

Cassin's Sparrow *(Aimophila cassinii)*

Fairly common summer resident. Very uncommon and local in winter. This species apparently responds to the midsummer wet season that usually occurs in the Trans-Pecos during early to mid-July. Cassin's Sparrow may be quite visible from early March to mid-May and then again from July through October when seasonal afternoon showers begin. It is shy and retiring in winter.

Rufous-crowned Sparrow *(Aimophila ruficeps)*

Common to fairly common permanent resident in mountains and foothills.

American Tree Sparrow *(Spizella arborea)*

Casual winter visitor. Most sightings are from Guadalupe Mountains National Park. Two records from Hueco Tanks State Park.

Chipping Sparrow *(Spizella passerina)*

Abundant to fairly common migrant. Common to uncommon in winter. Very common summer resident in the high woodlands of the Davis and Guadalupe mountains.

Clay-colored Sparrow *(Spizella pallida)*

Fairly common to uncommon migrant (rare in western third of Trans-Pecos) with more records from fall than spring. Population may fluctuate in winter, when it is generally very rare, but these birds can occasionally reach "uncommon" status at this season around Big Bend National Park. Usually found at lower elevations.

Brewer's Sparrow *(Spizella breweri)*

Common to uncommon migrant and winter resident.

Field Sparrow *(Spizella pusilla)*

Uncommon to very rare migrant and winter resident. Occasionally absent altogether during midwinter. There have been recent reports from the eastern Trans-Pecos during spring and early summer, but there are no indications of breeding at this writing.

Black-chinned Sparrow *(Spizella atrogularis)*

Uncommon winter resident in open mountain canyons and nearby washes. Locally common breeding species at scattered locations in grassy mountain meadows above 4,500 ft.

Vesper Sparrow *(Pooecetes gramineus)*

Uncommon winter resident. Fairly common to uncommon migrant.

Lark Sparrow *(Chondestes grammacus)*

Common to uncommon migrant and summer resident. Very rare to casual in winter. This species does not breed around Big Bend National Park and is a locally uncommon breeding bird in El Paso and Hudspeth counties. In general, however, this is a common breeding bird throughout most of the Trans-Pecos.

Black-chinned Sparrow

Black-throated Sparrow *(Amphispiza bilineata)*

Abundant to common permanent resident. One of the most frequently seen birds in desert shrub habitat.

Sage Sparrow *(Amphispiza belli)*

Uncommon and local winter resident. Very irregular. During some winters, this bird can be locally fairly common in sandy sagebrush-type flats from around Big Bend country to the north and west toward New Mexico. Most winters it is rare in the Trans-Pecos except around El Paso, where it is considered uncommon.

Lark Bunting *(Calamospiza melanocorys)*

Very common to fairly common migrant and winter resident.

Black-throated Sparrow

Numbers vary from year to year. One nest record from northern Brewster County near the town of Alpine.

Savannah Sparrow *(Passerculus sandwichensis)*

Common to uncommon migrant and winter resident.

Baird's Sparrow *(Ammodramus bairdii)*

Very rare in fall, winter, and spring. Found in the grasslands of the Trans-Pecos, with most records coming from Brewster, Jeff Davis, and Presidio counties. Although this bird is a review species, most sightings are not submitted to the TBRC. There are currently over one hundred reports unsubmitted for review. *Review Species.*

Grasshopper Sparrow *(Ammodramus savannarum)*

Uncommon to casual migrant and winter resident and a locally uncommon breeding bird. This species is an uncommon summer resident in the grasslands around Valentine, Marfa, and Alpine, Texas. Very irregular in most of the Trans-Pecos.

LeConte's Sparrow *(Ammodramus leconteii)*

Casual migrant and winter visitor. Observations from Brewster and Reeves counties.

Nelson's Sharp-tailed Sparrow *(Ammodramus nelsoni)*

Accidental. One record from Lake Balmorhea (photograph, TPRF #221 [1980]). The sighting of this species is presumed based on the recent A.O.U. split of *Ammodramus caudacutus*. The Saltmarsh Sharp-tailed Sparrow (*A. caudacutus*) is a bird of northeastern salt marshes, while Nelson's Sharp-tailed Sparrow nests in the prairie states and is generally found in winter along the Gulf Coast and in southern Atlantic states.

Fox Sparrow *(Passerella iliaca)*

Rare migrant and winter visitor. It appears that the majority of records are of the rusty eastern race.

Song Sparrow *(Melospiza melodia)*

Common to uncommon migrant and winter resident. More often observed in the northern Trans-Pecos.

Lincoln's Sparrow *(Melospiza lincolnii)*

Common to fairly common migrant and winter resident.

Swamp Sparrow *(Melospiza georgiana)*

Fairly common to uncommon migrant and winter resident. Somewhat localized, usually around wet seeps, streamsides, small ponds, and lakes.

White-throated Sparrow *(Zonotrichia albicollis)*

Rare to uncommon migrant and winter resident.

Harris's Sparrow *(Zonotrichia querula)*

Casual winter visitor. Scattered sightings throughout the Trans-

Pecos ranging from mid-November to mid-March. There are several records of lone birds found within large flocks of White-crowned Sparrows.

White-crowned Sparrow *(Zonotrichia leucophrys)*

Abundant to common migrant and winter resident.

Golden-crowned Sparrow *(Zonotrichia atricapilla)*

Casual fall and winter visitor, with six accepted records. Although most records are from November and December, one sighting from Hueco Tanks State Park remained from December 24, 1993, through May of 1994 and apparently returned for the following two winters into 1996. Other sightings are from El Paso, Big Bend National Park, Guadalupe Mountains National Park, Valentine, and Davis Mountains State Park. *Review Species.*

Dark-eyed Junco *(Junco hyemalis)*

Common to fairly common migrant and winter resident. The "Gray-headed Junco" is a fairly common nester in the Guadalupe Mountains, but nesting is not confirmed elsewhere in the Trans-Pecos. In migration and winter other forms of these species are common to uncommon; only the "slate-colored" is considered rare.

Yellow-eyed Junco *(Junco phaeonotus)*

Casual. Five well-documented records. Three records are from Guadalupe Mountains National Park (November 27, 1987, March 20–early April, 1988, and November 25, 1996). The 1988 record includes a photograph (TPRF #660). Two records are from Big Bend National Park (June 17, 1980, and April 25–May 5, 1990). One recently submitted El Paso record is currently under review. This bird nests in the high country of the Sierra Del Carmen Mountains 50 miles to the south of Big Bend National Park. *Review Species.*

McCown's Longspur *(Calcarius mccownii)*

Rare winter visitor in the central and northern Trans-Pecos. The largest flock reported was from Hudspeth County and contained over two hundred birds. Most often observed in short-grass areas, bare dirt fields, and sod farms. This species normally does not frequent the tall grasslands that the Chestnut-collared Longspur favors.

Lapland Longspur *(Calcarius lapponicus)*

Accidental in winter. Most records are from the northern Trans-Pecos.

Smith's Longspur *(Calcarius pictus)*

Accidental. One record from the grasslands in north El Paso County (November 22, 1985) and one from Big Bend National Park (April 29, 1986).

Chestnut-collared Longspur *(Calcarius ornatus)*

Uncommon to rare migrant and winter resident. Large flocks (three hundred birds) have been reported from the central and northern Trans-Pecos. Very small flocks or single individuals are irregularly reported from Big Bend country. As a general rule, this species prefers tall grasslands.

Snow Bunting *(Plectrophenax nivalis)*

Accidental in winter and spring. One record from Big Bend National Park (May 9, 1988) and a record of two individuals seen at Lake Balmorhea (November 27, 1993). *Review Species.*

CARDINALS AND GROSBEAKS: Family Cardinalidae

Northern Cardinal *(Cardinalis cardinalis)*

Fairly common resident, but the status of this bird varies somewhat. In much of the Trans-Pecos, the Northern Cardinal prefers areas near water, while the closely related Pyrrhuloxia prefers the dry scrubland. This species is quite rare in El Paso and Hudspeth counties but is considered generally common in the far southeastern Trans-Pecos in Val Verde County.

Pyrrhuloxia *(Cardinalis sinuatus)*

Common winter resident. Common to uncommon summer resident. Even though most Pyrrhuloxias appear to be year-round residents, there is some movement of birds in spring and summer. They are generally found in dry desert lowlands.

Rose-breasted Grosbeak *(Pheucticus ludovicianus)*

Rare spring migrant. Casual in fall. This species is seen with some regularity in small numbers every spring in the Trans-Pecos.

Black-headed Grosbeak *(Pheucticus melanocephalus)*

Common summer resident in the mountains of the Trans-Pecos. Fairly common to uncommon migrant in other areas. This species prefers wooded foothill canyons over high coniferous forest.

Blue Grosbeak *(Guiraca caerulea)*

Common migrant and summer resident. Casual in winter. Prefers scrubbier habitat than other grosbeaks.

Lazuli Bunting *(Passerina amoena)*

Fairly common to rare migrant. More common as a fall migrant from August to early September. One winter record (December 26, 1986–January 6, 1987) from El Paso.

Indigo Bunting *(Passerina cyanea)*

Rare migrant. Rare, localized breeding bird. This species nests irregularly along the Rio Grande, in lower canyons in the Chisos Mountains, and in El Paso County.

Varied Bunting *(Passerina versicolor)*

Fairly common to uncommon migrant and summer resident in Big Bend country east to Terrell County. Casual in winter. This bird is only occasionally seen outside of Big Bend country, with scattered records from Lake Balmorhea, the Davis Mountains, and even the Guadalupe Mountains. There are no records from Hudspeth County and only one record from El Paso County. Varied Buntings can reach common status in wet years around Big Bend National Park and Big Bend Ranch.

Painted Bunting *(Passerina ciris)*

Locally common to uncommon migrant and summer resident. This bird can be common along river thickets in willow and salt cedar but is generally uncommon, or even absent, throughout much of the Trans-Pecos. During fall migration, this bird's distribution is more homogeneous, and individuals may turn up in a variety of habitats.

Dickcissel *(Spiza americana)*

Uncommon to rare fall migrant. Somewhat irregular in much of the

Trans-Pecos. Frequently seen in very small flocks. Suspected of breeding in El Paso County in 1986.

BLACKBIRDS: Family Icteridae

Bobolink *(Dolichonyx oryzivorus)*

Accidental. Mid-May records exist for El Paso County (TPRF #466 [1976]) and Reeves County (TPRF #820 [1990]).

Red-winged Blackbird *(Agelaius phoeniceus)*

Common to fairly common permanent resident in most counties. Uncommon in Big Bend country and rare in much of the Guadalupe Mountains National Park.

Eastern Meadowlark *(Sturnella magna)*

Uncommon and local permanent resident in most counties. Uncommon migrant and winter visitor (but does not nest) in Big Bend country. This species, however, is the nesting meadowlark in the Davis Mountains and on the outskirts of Guadalupe Mountains National Park. Recent indications suggest that a third species of North American meadowlark may be present in the Trans-Pecos. This species (currently a subspecies) is sometimes referred to as "Lillian's" Meadowlark *(S. magna lillianae)*. It differs mainly in voice, but there are minor physical differences as well. It appears to be fairly common in the grasslands, where it likely replaces *S. m. magna*. If *S. m. lillianae* becomes a full species, then the status of *Sturnella magna* in the Trans-Pecos will need to be reevaluated.

Western Meadowlark *(Sturnella neglecta)*

Common to fairly common permanent resident in the northwest Trans-Pecos. Common to fairly common winter resident and uncommon summer resident in the southern and eastern Trans-Pecos.

Yellow-headed Blackbird *(Xanthocephalus xanthocephalus)*

Fairly common migrant and winter resident in El Paso and Hudspeth counties. There are at least two major roost sites in El Paso which in winter contain up to ten thousand birds each. Uncommon to rare wintering bird in most of the southern and eastern Trans-

Pecos. There are no recent nest records in the Trans-Pecos, although Oberholser lists one historical nest record for Culberson County (1939). Nonbreeders are uncommon to rare in summer in El Paso and Hudspeth counties but are generally absent at that time of year elsewhere in the Trans-Pecos.

Rusty Blackbird *(Euphagus carolinus)*

Casual winter visitor. Sightings are from Brewster, Hudspeth, and El Paso counties and range from October 24 to March 28. Most observations are from midwinter.

Brewer's Blackbird *(Euphagus cyanocephalus)*

Abundant to common migrant and winter resident in most of the Trans-Pecos. Fairly common migrant and rare winter visitor to Big Bend country and to Guadalupe Mountains National Park. One historical nest record from the Davis Mountains (July 18, 1969).

Common Grackle *(Quiscalus quiscula)*

Uncommon to very rare winter visitor. Locally uncommon breeding bird around Lake Balmorhea. Most observations are still of individual birds, but large flocks have been observed in the cities of Del Rio and, rarely, El Paso.

Great-tailed Grackle *(Quiscalus mexicanus)*

Abundant permanent resident around cities such as Alpine, Del Rio, and El Paso. Uncommon visitor in Big Bend National Park, where there is one nest record from Rio Grande Village (1983). It is rare in the Guadalupe Mountains. In general, this bird is rare at high elevations or in remote desert wilderness and quite common in low, populated areas.

Bronzed Cowbird *(Molothrus aeneus)*

Fairly common to rare summer resident. Since 1969, when it first arrived in Big Bend country, this species has increased rapidly from the southern to the northern Trans-Pecos. It is now an uncommon summer resident in El Paso. It is most commonly seen in Big Bend country and in the western Trans-Pecos.

Brown-headed Cowbird *(Molothrus ater)*

Common migrant and summer resident. Uncommon to rare in

winter, mostly around stockyards and feedlots. Generally found throughout the Trans-Pecos.

Black-vented Oriole *(Icterus wagleri)*

Accidental. One record from Big Bend National Park, which was observed over the course of three summers, 1968–1970. This bird was banded and photographed (TPRF #31) by R. H. Wauer. It was the first documented record of this bird for the United States. Review Species.

Orchard Oriole *(Icterus spurius)*

Fairly common migrant and summer resident in the southern Trans-Pecos. May be declining. Locally uncommon to rare in El Paso and Hudspeth counties and generally absent in the Guadalupe Mountains.

Hooded Oriole *(Icterus cucullatus)*

Locally fairly common to rare migrant and summer resident. This species appears to be declining along the Rio Grande floodplain around Big Bend National Park and is now uncommon. It is uncommon and local around the city of El Paso, and the species is considered accidental within Guadalupe Mountains National Park.

Baltimore Oriole *(Icterus galbula)*

Casual visitor. The Baltimore Oriole is easily separated in the field from the recently split Bullock's Oriole and has been observed at several locations within the Trans-Pecos. Observations are scattered from April 29 to August 28.

Bullock's Oriole *(Icterus bullockii)*

Locally fairly common to uncommon migrant and summer resident. Casual in winter. Although this species is more widespread in migration than the Hooded Oriole, it is equally spotty in its nesting habits. Most nest records are from El Paso, Hudspeth, and Culberson counties. Bullock's Oriole as a full species is a direct result of a 1996 A.O.U. split of the Northern Oriole.

Scott's Oriole *(Icterus parisorum)*

Common spring migrant and summer resident. Normally found in the yucca grasslands and oak foothills. Less common in fall and casual in winter. Irregular in the east toward Val Verde County.

FINCHES: Family Fringillidae

Purple Finch *(Carpodacus purpureus)*

Accidental. One photograph record (TPRF #222, December 30, 1980) from Big Bend National Park and one record of a female in El Paso County (October 15, 1982). Also, a historical record of a specimen taken from El Paso County on March 31, 1888. In invasion years, Purple Finches are frequently reported from the Trans-Pecos. However, there is little documentation that would separate Cassin's Finches from these sightings. The authors believe Purple Finches may have invaded the Trans-Pecos during certain years, but more thorough documentation is needed in order to determine status.

Cassin's Finch *(Carpodacus cassinii)*

Locally uncommon and irregular migrant and winter visitor. Cassin's Finch is seen with some regularity in the Guadalupe Mountains National Park during winter and spring with some lingering until June. Rare and irregular elsewhere. There have been "invasionary" seasons (usually November–March) such as 1996–1997, when Cassin's Finch, Red Crossbill, Lawrence's Goldfinch, and Evening Grosbeak were seen rather frequently at scattered locations throughout the Trans-Pecos.

House Finch *(Carpodacus mexicanus)*

Abundant to common permanent resident throughout.

Red Crossbill *(Loxia curvirostra)*

Locally uncommon and irregular permanent resident. Numbers vary widely. As a nesting species, it can be fairly common above 6,500 ft. in the Guadalupe Mountains during good years. There are only a few nest records for the Davis Mountains, and, although there are midsummer sightings in the Chisos Mountains, no documented nest records exist for that mountain range. In invasionary winters, this bird is possible in any coniferous forest and even into suburban neighborhoods with pine trees.

Pine Siskin *(Carduelis pinus)*

Common to fairly common migrant and winter resident. There are several summer sightings, but most of these are of single individuals that appear to be lingering. Oberholser lists two historical nest records: one from the Bowl in the Guadalupe Mountains (July 11, 1938) and one record in Madera Canyon in the Davis Mountains (June 6, 1970).

Lesser Goldfinch *(Carduelis psaltria)*

Common to fairly common migrant and summer resident in most of the Trans-Pecos. Uncommon in winter. This species is a rare and local breeding bird in El Paso and Hudspeth counties but is generally fairly common elsewhere as a breeding bird.

Lawrence's Goldfinch *(Carduelis lawrencei)*

Casual. Several recent records exist from the Trans-Pecos. There are one photograph record from Hueco Tanks State Park (TPRF #533, December 7, 1984) and one detailed account from Fort Bliss Sewage Ponds (February 11, 1996), both from El Paso County. There was an invasion of several birds beginning on October 12, 1996, when four birds were seen at Hueco Tanks, a single individual was observed at Fort Bliss, and a lone male was sighted in the Davis Mountains. Observations increased and birds lingered at scattered locations throughout the fall and winter season. There have been several historical sightings between 1934 and 1954, all between the months of November and March. *Review Species.*

American Goldfinch *(Carduelis tristis)*

Fairly common to uncommon migrant and winter resident.

Evening Grosbeak *(Coccothraustes vespertina)*

Very rare migrant and winter visitor. Most sightings are from the Guadalupe and Davis mountains.

House Sparrow *(Passer domesticus)*

Abundant to common permanent resident.

HYPOTHETICAL FOR THE TRANS-PECOS

Red-necked Grebe *(Podiceps grisegena)*

Oberholser lists one sight report (1936) from El Paso County. There is one other published reference to a sighting at Lake Balmorhea, but no solid documentation exists for this species in the Trans-Pecos. A potential record from Imperial Reservoir is under review.

Anhinga *(Anhinga anhinga)*

This species is fairly common along the Rio Grande in south Texas, and there are sightings from Big Bend National Park and Lake Amistad. However, documentation for this bird in the Trans-Pecos (including Val Verde County) is very weak. All observations located by the authors were of "fly-overs" and could have been misidentified cormorants.

Black Swift *(Cypseloides niger)*

A few sight records (one from El Paso is currently under review), but this species is hypothetical for the state and more documentation is needed. The Black Swift's wintering ground in Central America and the West Indies would certainly suggest migration through Texas, yet no specimens, photographs, or thorough written documentation exists.

Gray-cheeked Thrush *(Catharus minimus)*

There are scattered Big Bend sightings from the 1970's and four historical observations, but there is no well-written documentation anywhere that the authors have seen. Although some reports may be true, the frequent misidentification with other catharus thrushes (and even thrashers) makes this species suspect.

Bridled Titmouse *(Baeolophus wollweberi)*

There are two separate sightings in the year 1975 (R. H. Wauer) from Big Bend National Park and a total of three for the year 1981. None was submitted for review. All three sightings in 1981 were from the Basin area in Big Bend National Park, which included at least two individual birds and were reported by three separate parties over six months' time. This information suggests that Bridled Titmouse may have invasion years in the Trans-Pecos. However, there are no well-documented records for the state, and full acceptance as a Texas species will require more substantial evidence.

White-collared Seedeater *(Sporophila torqueola)*

One bird was photographed at the Fort Bliss Sewage Ponds (El Paso County, 1989). This record was not accepted by the TBRC because of questions about its origin (although it was of the western Mexican race, which would occur closest to El Paso).

SPECIES EXTIRPATED FROM THE TRANS-PECOS

Lesser Prairie-Chicken *(Tympanuchus pallidicinctus)*

Oberholser lists a specimen taken from Pecos County (1904) and sight records from Jeff Davis County. Loss of appropriate habitat is likely not to allow this species to regain a foothold in the Trans-Pecos.

INTRODUCED SPECIES

Ring-necked Pheasant *(Phasianus colchicus)*

Oberholser lists historical pheasant introductions by Texas Parks and Wildlife at Lake Balmorhea and El Paso that apparently have declined dramatically or perhaps are gone entirely. There are a few recent sightings around the Guadalupe Mountains, but these may be introductions from New Mexico or possibly introductions by local ranchers.

Chukar *(Alectoris chukar)*

Introduced species in northern Brewster County, with over one hundred birds released in 1969. There no longer appears to be a substantial population remaining anywhere in the Trans-Pecos.

THE SEASONAL DISTRIBUTION
OF TRANS-PECOS BIRDS

The following list shows the seasonal status and distribution of Trans-Pecos birds. Because of the enormous size of the Trans-Pecos and the varied geography, the distribution of a bird species may vary greatly from one compass point to another. In this list, a term such as common is more easily defined if it is associated with the location where it is most often observed. In the chart below, if this "most often observed" category is left blank, then that species has shown no historical preference for any one particular area of the Trans-Pecos.

Although the following Table 2 uses absolute values for each season based largely on written records, the reader should be aware that these seasonal notations are general in nature. Unpredictable factors such as seasonal rainfall and food availability still play a major role in the status and distribution of Trans-Pecos birds. The following chart reflects overall species abundance during what can only be called "average" years.

LEGEND

Ab	Abundant: Should see on every trip in the proper habitat.
C	Common: Should see on 3 out of 4 trips in the proper habitat.
FC	Fairly Common: Should see on 2 out of 4 trips in the proper habitat.
U	Uncommon: Should see on 1 out of 4 trips in the proper habitat.
R	Rare: Should see on 1 out of 10 trips or less in the proper habitat.
Ca	Casual: Not expected annually and includes out-of-season occurrences. Generally refers to 10 records or fewer for the region.

Ac	Accidental: Generally refers to 3 records or fewer for the region.
?	Questionable: Status not entirely known.
(ir)	Very irregular. May not occur year after year.
(L)	Occurs locally within a limited geographical or altitudinal range.
(H)	Historical records only (prior to 1974).
(ab)	Completely absent throughout some geographical areas in the Trans-Pecos but observed regularly in others.
BB	Big Bend country. Generally the southern three-quarters of Brewster and Presidio counties.
NO	Northern Trans-Pecos (from the Davis Mountains north).
VA	Val Verde County and the southeastern Trans-Pecos.
DM	Davis Mountains.
GU	Guadalupe Mountains.
CH	Chisos Mountains.
MT	Normally found in the major mountain ranges.
RG	The Rio Grande watershed.

SEASONAL DEFINITIONS

Spring	March through May
Summer	June through Mid-August
Fall	Mid-August through Mid-November
Winter	Mid-November through February

TABLE 2

THE SEASONAL DISTRIBUTION OF TRANS-PECOS BIRDS

BIRDS OF THE TRANS-PECOS	SPRING	SUMMER
Red-throated Loon	Ac	
Pacific Loon	Ac	
Common Loon		
Yellow-billed Loon		
Least Grebe	R - Ca	
Pied-billed Grebe	FC	U
Horned Grebe	R	
Eared Grebe	FC	U (L)
Western Grebe	R	(ir)
Clark's Grebe	R	(ir)
American White Pelican	U - R	Ac
Brown Pelican	Ac	Ca
Double-crested Cormorant	C	R
Neotropic Cormorant	FC - R	FC - R
American Bittern	R	
Least Bittern	R	R
Great Blue Heron	C	U
Great Egret	U	U
Snowy Egret	FC	FC
Little Blue Heron	R	R
Tricolored Heron	R	R
Reddish Egret	Ac	Ca
Cattle Egret	FC	C
Green Heron	FC	FC
Black-crowned Night-Heron	FC	U
Yellow-crowned Night-Heron	Ca	Ca

FALL	WINTER	NESTS	MOST OFTEN OBSERVED	REVIEW SPECIES
Ac	Ca			X
Ac	Ca			
R	R			
	Ac			X
	R - Ca		VA, RG	
FC	FC	x (L)		
R	Ca			
FC	FC	x (L)		
FC-U	FC - U	x (L) (ir)		
U - R	U - R	x (L) (ir)		
U - R	R (ir)			
Ca	Ac			
C	C	x (L)	(ab)	
FC - R	U - R (L)	x (L)	VA, NO	
R	Ca		RG	
		x		
C	C	x (H)		
U	U	x (L)		
FC	R	x (L)		
R	Ca			
R				
Ca				
FC	U	x (L)		
FC	U - R	x (L)		
FC	U - R	x (L)		
Ca				

BIRDS OF THE TRANS-PECOS	SPRING	SUMMER
White Ibis	Ac	Ac
Glossy Ibis	Ac	
White-faced Ibis	FC	FC - U
Roseate Spoonbill		Ca
Wood Stork		Ca
Black Vulture	C (L)	C (L)
Turkey Vulture	C	C
Black-bellied Whistling Duck	U (L)	U (L)
Fulvous-Whistling Duck	Ca	Ca
Greater White-fronted Goose	R	
Snow Goose	U	Ca
Ross' Goose	R	Ca
Canada Goose	U	
Tundra Swan	Ca	
Wood Duck	U (L)	U (L)
Gadwall	C - FC	R
Eurasian Wigeon	Ca	
American Wigeon	C	Ca
Mallard	C - FC	C - FC
Blue-winged Teal	FC	R
Cinnamon Teal	FC	U - R
Northern Shoveler	Ab - FC	R (L)
Northern Pintail	U	R
Garganey	Ac	
Green-winged Teal	Ab - C	R
Canvasback	R	Ca
Redhead	FC - Ca	U
Ring-necked Duck	FC - R	Ca

FALL	WINTER	NESTS	MOST OFTEN OBSERVED	REVIEW SPECIES
	Ac			
FC	Ca	x (L)		
Ca				
C (L)	C (L)	x (L)	VA	
C	U - Ca	x		
R	Ac	x (L)	VA	
R	R			
U	U			
R	U - R		NO	
U	U			
Ca	Ca			
U (L)	U (L)	x	RG	
C - FC	C - FC			
	Ca		NO	X
C	Ab - U			
C - FC	C - FC	x		
FC	Ac	x (ir)		
FC	U - R	x		
Ab - FC	Ab - FC	x (ir)		
C	C	x (ir)		
				X
Ab - C	Ab - C			
R	FC - U			
FC - Ca	FC - Ca	x (L)		
FC - Ca	FC - Ca			

BIRDS OF THE TRANS-PECOS	SPRING	SUMMER
Greater Scaup		
Lesser Scaup	FC - R	Ca
Surf Scoter	Ac	
White-winged Scoter		
Black Scoter		
Oldsquaw	Ca	
Common Goldeneye		
Barrow's Goldeneye		
Hooded Merganser		
Red-breasted Merganser		
Common Merganser	R	Ac
Bufflehead	U - R	Ca
Masked Duck		Ac
Ruddy Duck	FC - U	U (L)
Osprey	U	
Swallow-tailed Kite		Ac
White-tailed Kite	Ca	Ca
Mississippi Kite	U	U
Bald Eagle		
Northern Harrier	FC	Ca
Sharp-shinned Hawk	FC	Ca
Cooper's Hawk	FC	R
Northern Goshawk		
Gray Hawk	U	U
Common Black-Hawk	R - Ca	R (L)
Harris's Hawk	FC (L)	FC (L)
Red-shouldered Hawk	Ca	Ca
Broad-winged Hawk	R	

FALL	WINTER	NESTS	MOST OFTEN OBSERVED	REVIEW SPECIES
	R		NO	
FC - R	FC - R			
Ca	Ac			
Ac				
Ac	Ac			
Ac	Ca		NO	
	U - R		NO, VA	
	Ac			X
	R			
U - R	U - R		NO, VA	
R	U		NO	
FC - U	FC - U			
				X
FC - U	FC - U	x (L)		
U	R			
Ac				
U		x (L)		
	R - Ca			
FC	FC	x (H)		
FC	FC	x		
FC	FC	x		
	Ac			X
		x	BB (ab)	
Ca		x (L)	DA (ab)	
FC (L)	FC (L)	x	VA, NO (ab)	
Ca	Ca	x	VA, BB (ab)	
R				

BIRDS OF THE TRANS-PECOS	SPRING	SUMMER
Swainson's Hawk	FC	FC - R
White-tailed Hawk	Ac	Ac
Zone-tailed Hawk	U	U
Red-tailed Hawk	Ab	FC - U
Ferruginous Hawk		
Rough-legged Hawk		
Golden Eagle	U	U
Crested Caracara	R	R
American Kestrel	Ab - C	FC - U
Merlin	R	
Aplomado Falcon	Ac	
Prairie Falcon	U	U
Peregrine Falcon	U - R	U - R
Wild Turkey	U - R	U - R
Montezuma Quail	FC (L)	FC (L)
Northern Bobwhite	C (L)	C (L)
Scaled Quail	C	C
Gambel's Quail	C (L)	C (L)
Yellow Rail	Ac	
King Rail	R	R
Virginia Rail	U	U - R
Sora	FC	R
Purple Gallinule	R - Ca	R - Ca
Common Moorhen	FC - R	FC - R
American Coot	C - FC	C - R
Sandhill Crane		
Black-bellied Plover	R	Ca
American Golden-Plover	Ac	
Snowy Plover	FC - R	U

FALL	WINTER	NESTS	MOST OFTEN OBSERVED	REVIEW SPECIES
FC		x	NO	
U		x	BB, DA (ab)	
Ab	Ab	x		
U	U			
	R - Ca			
U	U	x		
R	R		VA (ab)	
Ab - C	Ab - C	x		
R	R			
	Ac			
U	U	x (L)		
U - R	R	x (L)		
U - R	U - R	x	(ab)	
FC (L)	FC (L)	x (L)	DA (ab)	
C (L)	C (L)	x (L)	VA (ab)	
C	C	x		
C (L)	C (L)	x (L)	NO, RG (ab)	
	Ac			
		x (ir)		
U - R	R	x		
FC	U	x		
			BB, VA	
FC - R	FC - R	x	NO	
C - FC	Ab - U	x		
U	R			
R				
Ca				
FC - R	R	x (L)	NO, VA	

BIRDS OF THE TRANS-PECOS	SPRING	SUMMER
Semipalmated Plover	U	U
Piping Plover		
Killdeer	C - U	C - U
Mountain Plover		R
Black-necked Stilt	C - R	U - R
American Avocet	FC - U	FC - U
Northern Jacana		
Greater Yellowlegs	FC - U	FC - U
Lesser Yellowlegs	FC - U	FC - U
Solitary Sandpiper	FC - U	FC - U
Willet	U	R
Spotted Sandpiper	C	U
Upland Sandpiper	R	
Whimbrel	Ca	
Long-billed Curlew	U	Ca
Hudsonian Godwit	Ac	Ac
Marbled Godwit	U - R	Ca
Ruddy Turnstone	Ca	
Red Knot	Ca	
Sanderling	Ca	
Semipalmated Sandpiper	R	R
Western Sandpiper	C - FC	R
Red-necked Stint		Ac
Least Sandpiper	Ab - FC	R
White-rumped Sandpiper	R	
Baird's Sandpiper	U	
Pectoral Sandpiper	R	
Dunlin		

FALL	WINTER	NESTS	MOST OFTEN OBSERVED	REVIEW SPECIES
U	Ac			
Ac				
C - U	C - U	x		
Ac			NO (ab)	
C - R	R (L)	x		
FC - U	Ca	x		
Ac				X
FC - U	U			
FC - U	R			
FC - U				
R			NO (ab)	
C	FC - U			
U (L)				
			NO	
U	R			
R			NO (ab)	
Ca			NO (ab)	
Ca			NO (ab)	
R			NO (ab)	
U - R			NO (ab)	
C - FC	R - Ca			
				X
Ab - FC	FC -U			
Ca			NO (ab)	
FC - U			NO	
U			NO	
R	Ca		NO (ab)	

BIRDS OF THE TRANS-PECOS	SPRING	SUMMER
Stilt Sandpiper	R	
Ruff		Ac
Short-billed Dowitcher		
Long-billed Dowitcher	FC - R	
Common Snipe	FC - U	
American Woodcock		
Wilson's Phalarope	C - U	U
Red-necked Phalarope	Ca	
Red Phalarope		
Parasitic Jaeger		
Long-tailed Jaeger		Ac
Laughing Gull	R	R
Franklin's Gull	FC - R	Ca
Bonaparte's Gull	R	
Mew Gull		
Ring-billed Gull	FC	R
California Gull	Ac	Ac
Herring Gull	R	
Thayer's Gull		
Lesser Black-backed Gull		
Western Gull	Ac	Ac
Black-legged Kittiwake		
Sabine's Gull	Ac	
Caspian Tern		Ca
Elegant Tern		
Common Tern	R - Ca	
Arctic Tern		Ac
Forster's Tern	FC	

FALL	WINTER	NESTS	MOST OFTEN OBSERVED	REVIEW SPECIES
FC - R			NO (ab)	
				X
R - Ca			NO	
FC - R	U - R			
FC - U	FC - U			
Ca	Ac			
C - U				
U - Ca			NO (ab)	
Ca			NO (ab)	X
	Ac			
				X
R		x		
R	Ca			
FC - U	Ca			
	Ac			X
FC	FC			
Ac	Ca		NO	X
R	R			
	Ac			X
	Ac			X
				X
	Ca			X
Ca			NO	X
Ca			NO	
	Ac			X
R			NO	
				X
FC	Ca			

BIRDS OF THE TRANS-PECOS	SPRING	SUMMER
Least Tern	R	U (L)
Sooty Tern		Ac
Black Tern	U - FC	U - R
Black Skimmer		Ac
Rock Dove	Ab (L)	Ab (L)
Band-tailed Pigeon	FC	FC
White-winged Dove	C - FC	C - FC
Mourning Dove	Ab - C	Ab - C
Inca Dove	C (L)	C (L)
Common Ground-Dove	U - R	U - R
Ruddy Ground-Dove	Ac	
White-tipped Dove		Ac
Monk Parakeet	U (L)	U (L)
Black-billed Cuckoo		
Yellow-billed Cuckoo	FC - U	FC - U
Greater Roadrunner	FC	FC
Groove-billed Ani	FC - R	FC - R
Barn Owl	FC - U	FC - U
Flammulated Owl	FC - U	FC - U
Eastern Screech-Owl	U - R	U - R
Western Screech-Owl	C - R	C - R
Great Horned Owl	FC	FC
Northern Pygmy Owl	Ac	Ac
Elf Owl	C - FC	C - FC
Burrowing Owl	FC	FC
Spotted Owl	R (L)	R (L)
Barred Owl	U	U
Long-eared Owl	R (ir)	
Short-eared Owl	Ac	

FALL	WINTER	NESTS	MOST OFTEN OBSERVED	REVIEW SPECIES
R		x (L)	VA, RG	
U - FC			NO	
Ab (L)	Ab (L)	x		
FC	U	x	MT	
C - FC	U (L)	x		
Ab - C	C - FC	x		
C (L)	C (L)	x (L)		
U - R	R	x (L)	BB (ab)	
	Ac			X
Ac				
U (L)	U (L)	x (L)	NO (ab)	
Ac				
FC - U		x		
FC	FC	x		
Ca	Ca	x	VA, BB (ab)	
FC - U	FC - U	x	NO	
FC - U	FC - U	x	MT	
U - R	U - R	x	VA (ab)	
C - R	C - R	x	BB	
FC	FC	x		
				X
C - FC	Ac	x	BB (ab)	
FC	R (L)	x	NO	
R (L)	R (L)	x (L)	GU, DA	
U	U	x	VA (ab)	
U - R (ir)	U - R (ir)		NO	
Ca (ir)	Ca (ir)			

BIRDS OF THE TRANS-PECOS	SPRING	SUMMER
Northern Saw-whet Owl	R	R
Lesser Nighthawk	C	C
Common Nighthawk	U	U
Pauraque	Ac	
Common Poorwill	C - FC	C - FC
Chuck-will's-widow		
Whip-poor-will	C - FC	C - FC
Chimney Swift	C (L)	C (L)
White-throated Swift	C - FC	C - FC
Broad-billed Hummingbird	Ca	Ca
White-eared Hummingbird	Ac	Ac
Berylline Hummingbird		Ac
Violet-crowned Hummingbird	Ac	
Blue-throated Hummingbird	FC	FC
Magnificent Hummingbird	U	U
Lucifer Hummingbird	FC (L)	FC (L)
Ruby-throated Hummingbird	R-Ca	R - Ca
Black-chinned Hummingbird	C	C
Anna's Hummingbird	R	Ca (ir)
Costa's Hummingbird	Ca	
Calliope Hummingbird		U - R
Broad-tailed Hummingbird	FC - U	C - U
Rufous Hummingbird	Ca	C
Allen's Hummigbird		Ac
Elegant Trogon	Ac	
Ringed Kingfisher	U	U
Belted Kingfisher	FC	R
Green Kingfisher	FC - R	FC - R

FALL	WINTER	NESTS	MOST OFTEN OBSERVED	REVIEW SPECIES
Ca	Ca	x	GU	X
R	Ca	x		
U		x (L)	GU, DA	
U	R	x		
Ac			VA (ab)	
U		x	MT (ab)	
C (L)		x	VA (ab)	
C - FC	U	x		
Ac	Ac	x (H)	BB, NO	X
Ac		(?)		X
				X
Ac	Ac			X
FC		x (L)	BB (ab)	
U		x (L)	MT (ab)	
FC (L)		x (L)	BB (ab)	
R - Ca			BB, DA	
C	Ac	x		
U - R	U - R	x (ir)		
Ac	Ca			X
U - R	Ac		NO	
FC - U	Ac	x	MT	
C	Ca			
				X
	Ac			X
		? (L)	VA (ab)	
FC	FC - U	? (L)		
FC - Ca	FC - Ca	x	VA (ab)	

BIRDS OF THE TRANS-PECOS	SPRING	SUMMER
Lewis's Woodpecker	Ca	
Red-headed Woodpecker	Ca	Ca
Acorn Woodpecker	C	C
Golden-fronted Woodpecker	C - U	C - U
Yellow-bellied Sapsucker	U - R	
Red-naped Sapsucker	FC - U	
Williamson's Sapsucker	R	
Ladder-backed Woodpecker	C - FC	C - FC
Downy Woodpecker	R - Ca	
Hairy Woodpecker	U (L)	FC - U (L)
Northern Flicker	C	FC - U
Tufted Flycatcher	Ac	
Olive-sided Flycatcher	U	R
Greater Pewee	Ac	Ac
Western Wood-Pewee	C	C
Eastern Wood-Pewee	U	U
Yellow-bellied Flycatcher		
Willow Flycatcher	FC - U	R
Least Flycatcher	FC - R	
Acadian Flycatcher		R
Hammond's Flycatcher	U	
Dusky Flycatcher	FC - U	
Gray Flycatcher	U - R	C (L)
Cordilleran Flycatcher	FC-U	U
Black Phoebe	C	FC - U
Eastern Phoebe	U - R	U - R
Say's Phoebe	C	FC
Vermilion Flycatcher	C - FC	C - FC

FALL	WINTER	NESTS	MOST OFTEN OBSERVED	REVIEW SPECIES
Ac	Ca			X
Ac				
C	C	x	MT	
C - U	C - U	x	VA, BB (ab)	
U - R	U - R			
FC - U	FC - U		MT	
R	R		MT (ab)	
C - FC	C - FC	x		
R - Ca	R - Ca			
U (L)	U (L)	x (L)	GU (ab)	
C	C	x		
	Ac			X
U		x (L)	GU	
	Ac			X
C		x		
U		x	VA (ab)	
Ac				
FC - U		x (H)		
FC - R			VA	
			VA	
U	Ac			
FC - U	R			
U - R	R	x (L)	DA	
FC-U		x	MT	
C	C	x		
U - R	U - R	x	VA	
C	C	x		
C - FC	U	x	BB	

BIRDS OF THE TRANS-PECOS	SPRING	SUMMER
Dusky-capped Flycatcher	Ca	R (L)
Ash-throated Flycatcher	C	C
Great-crested Flycatcher		
Brown-crested Flycatcher	FC - Ca	FC - Ca
Great Kiskadee	U	U
Sulphur-bellied Flycatcher		Ac
Tropical Kingbird		Ac
Couch's Kingbird	U	U
Cassin's Kingbird	C - FC	C - FC
Thick-billed Kingbird	R (ir)	R (ir)
Western Kingbird	C - R	C - R
Eastern Kingbird	R	R
Scissor-tailed Flycatcher	C - U	C - U
Rose-throated Becard		Ac
Northern Shrike		
Loggerhead Shrike	C - FC	FC - U
White-eyed Vireo	R	Ca
Bell's Vireo	C	C
Black-capped Vireo	R	R
Gray Vireo	U - R (L)	U - R (L)
Blue-headed Vireo	R	
Cassin's Vireo	U	
Plumbeous Vireo	FC	C
Yellow-throated Vireo	U (L)	U (L)
Hutton's Vireo	FC - U	FC
Warbling Vireo	C - FC	C (L)
Philadelphia Vireo	Ca	
Red-eyed Vireo	U - R	U (L)

FALL	WINTER	NESTS	MOST OFTEN OBSERVED	REVIEW SPECIES
Ca	Ca	x (L)	DA (ab)	X
U	R - Ca	x		
R				
		x	VA, RG (ab)	
U	R	x	VA (ab)	
			BB	X
				X
U		x	VA (ab)	
C - FC	Ac	x	DA, GU	
		x (ir) (L)	BB (ab)	X
C - R		x	NO, VA	
R			VA	
C - U		x	VA	
				X
	Ac			
C - FC	C	x		
	Ca		VA (ab)	
C	U	x	BB (ab)	
		x (L)	VA, BB (ab)	
U - R (L)	R (L)	x (L)	(ab)	
R	Ca			
U	R			
FC	R	x	MT	
U (L)		x (L)	VA (ab)	
FC - U	FC - U	x	CH, DA	
C - FC		x (L)	GU	
R				
U - R		x (L)	VA	

BIRDS OF THE TRANS-PECOS	SPRING	SUMMER
Yellow-green Vireo		Ac
Steller's Jay	C	C
Blue Jay		
Green Jay		
Western Scrub-Jay	C	C
Mexican Jay	C (L)	C (L)
Pinyon Jay		
Clark's Nutcracker	Ca	Ca
Black-billed Magpie		
American Crow	C - U (L)	C - U (L)
Chihuahuan Raven	FC	FC
Common Raven	C - U	C - U
Horned Lark	C - U	C (L)
Purple Martin	U	
Tree Swallow	FC - U	
Violet-green Swallow	FC - U	FC - U
Northern Rough-winged Swallow	FC	FC - U
Bank Swallow	FC - U	Ca (L)
Barn Swallow	FC - U	Ab - C
Cliff Swallow	C - FC	C
Cave Swallow	C - U	C
Carolina Chickadee		
Black-capped Chickadee	Ac (H)	
Mountain Chickadee	C - FC	C - FC
Juniper Titmouse	U (L)	U (L)
Tufted Titmouse	C	C
Verdin	C - U	C - U
Bushtit	C	C
Red-breasted Nuthatch	U - R (ir)	(L)

FALL	WINTER	NESTS	MOST OFTEN OBSERVED	REVIEW SPECIES
				X
C	C	x	DA, GU	
Ca (ir)	Ca (ir)			
	R (ir)		VA	
C	C	x	DA, GU	
C (L)	C (L)	x (L)	CH	
U - R (ir)	U - R (ir)		DA, GU	
	Ca		MT	X
	Ac			X
C - U (L)	C - U (L)	x (L)	NO, VA	
FC	FC	x		
C - U	C - U	x	MT	
C - U	C - FC	x (L)	(ab)	
U			VA (ab)	
FC - U	Ca			
FC - U		x	MT	
FC	R	x		
FC - U		x (L)		
FC - U		x		
C - FC		x		
C - FC	Ca (L)	x	NO	
	Ca			
				X
C - FC	C - FC	x	GU, DA	
U (L)	U (L)	x (L)	GU (ab)	
C	C	x	CH, DA (ab)	
C - U	C - U	x		
C	C	x	MT	
FC - R (ir)	FC - R (ir)	x (L)		

BIRDS OF THE TRANS-PECOS	SPRING	SUMMER
White-breasted Nuthatch	C - FC	C - FC
Pygmy Nuthatch	FC - U (L)	FC - U (L)
Brown Creeper	R	R
Cactus Wren	C	C
Rock Wren	C - FC	C - FC
Canyon Wren	C - FC	C - FC
Carolina Wren	U (L)	U (L)
Bewick's Wren	FC	FC - C
House Wren	FC	FC - R (L)
Winter Wren	R - Ca	
Sedge Wren	R - Ca	
Marsh Wren	C - FC	
American Dipper		
Golden-crowned Kinglet	R (ir)	
Ruby-crowned Kinglet	Ab - C	
Blue-gray Gnatcatcher	U	C (L)
Black-tailed Gnatcatcher	FC - R	FC - R
Eastern Bluebird	R - U	
Western Bluebird	C - FC	C - FC
Mountain Bluebird	FC - U	R (L)
Townsend's Solitaire	FC - U	
Veery	Ac	
Swainson's Thrush	R - U	
Hermit Thrush	C - FC	FC
Wood Thrush	Ca	
Rufous-backed Robin		
American Robin	FC	C - U (L)
Varied Thrush	Ca	
Aztec Thrush		Ac

FALL	WINTER	NESTS	MOST OFTEN OBSERVED	REVIEW SPECIES
C - FC	C - FC	x	MT	
FC - U	FC - U	x	GU, DA	
U - R	U - R	x (L)	GU	
C	C	x		
C - FC	C - FC	x		
C - FC	C - FC	x		
U (L)	U (L)	x	VA (ab)	
FC	FC	x		
FC	U	x (L)	GU, DA	
R - Ca	R - Ca			
R - Ca	R - Ca			
C - FC	C - FC	x (H)		
Ca	Ca			X
R (ir)	U - R (ir)		GU	
Ab - C	Ab - C			
U	R	x		
FC - R	FC - R	x	BB	
R - U	R - U	x (L)		
C - FC	C - FC	x	MT	
FC - U	FC - U	x (L)(ir)	DA, GU	
FC - U	FC - U		GU	
R - U			MT	
C - FC	U	x (L)		
Ac	Ac			
Ac	Ac			X
FC	FC	x (L)		
Ac	Ac			X
				X

BIRDS OF THE TRANS-PECOS	SPRING	SUMMER
Gray Catbird	Ca	Ac
Northern Mockingbird	C	Ab - C
Sage Thrasher	U	
Brown Thrasher	R	
Long-billed Thrasher	R - Ca	R - Ca
Curve-billed Thrasher	C - U	C - R
Crissal Thrasher	FC - U	FC - U
European Starling	C	C
American Pipit	C - FC	
Sprague's Pipit	Ca	
Cedar Waxwing	C - U	
Gray Silky-flycatcher		
Phainopepla	U	U
Olive Warbler	Ac	
Blue-winged Warbler	Ac	Ac
Golden-winged Warbler	Ca	
Tennessee Warbler	Ca	
Orange-crowned Warbler	FC	FC - R (L)
Nashville Warbler	U - R	
Virginia's Warbler	FC - U	FC - R (L)
Colima Warbler	C - FC	C - FC
Lucy's Warbler	R	U (L)
Crescent-chested Warbler		Ac
Northern Parula	R	Ca
Tropical Parula	Ac	
Yellow Warbler	FC	Ca
Chestnut-sided Warbler	Ca	
Magnolia Warbler	Ca	
Cape May Warbler	Ac	

FALL	WINTER	NESTS	MOST OFTEN OBSERVED	REVIEW SPECIES
Ca	Ca			
C	FC - U	x		
U	U			
R	R			
			VA (ab)	
C - U	C - U	x		
FC - U	FC - U	x	NO, BB	
C	C	x	VA, NO	
C - FC	C - FC			
Ca	Ca		BB, VA (ab)	
C - U	C - U (ir)			
	Ac			X
U	U	x	BB, DA	
				X
Ca				
FC	U	x (L)		
U - R				
FC - U		x (L)	GU	
U		x (L)	CH (ab)	
R	Ac	x (L)	RG (ab)	
				X
R	Ca			
FC	Ac	x (H)		
Ca				
Ca				

BIRDS OF THE TRANS-PECOS	SPRING	SUMMER
Black-throated Blue Warbler	Ca	Ac
Yellow-rumped Warbler	C	FC (L) ⸱
Black-throated Gray Warbler	U - R	
Townsend's Warbler	FC - U	
Hermit Warbler	R	
Black-throated Green Warbler	Ca	Ca
Golden-cheeked Warbler	Ac	Ac
Blackburnian Warbler	Ca	
Yellow-throated Warbler	Ca	
Grace's Warbler	R	C
Pine Warbler	Ca	
Prairie Warbler	Ac	Ac
Palm Warbler	Ca	
Bay-breasted Warbler	Ac	
Blackpoll Warbler	Ca	
Black and White Warbler	U - R	Ca
American Redstart	U - R	Ca
Prothonotary Warbler	Ca	
Worm-eating Warbler	R - Ca	
Swainson's Warbler	Ac	
Ovenbird	R	
Northern Waterthrush	R - U	
Louisiana Waterthrush	Ca	
Kentucky Warbler	Ca	
Mourning Warbler		
MacGillivray's Warbler	FC	Ca
Common Yellowthroat	FC	FC
Hooded Warbler	R	
Wilson's Warbler	Ab - C	

FALL	WINTER	NESTS	MOST OFTEN OBSERVED	REVIEW SPECIES
Ca				
C	C	x (L)		
U - R	Ca			
FC - U	Ca			
R	Ac			
Ca	Ac			
Ac				
Ca			VA	
R		x (L)	DA, GU	
Ac	Ac			
Ac				
Ca	Ac			
Ac	Ac			
U - R	Ca			
U - R	Ac			
Ca	Ac			
Ac				
R				
R - U				
Ca				
Ac				
FC				
FC	R - U	x	RG	
Ac				
Ab - C	Ca			

BIRDS OF THE TRANS-PECOS	SPRING	SUMMER
Canada Warbler	Ac	
Red-faced Warbler	Ca	Ca
Painted Redstart	R (L)	R (L)
Slate-throated Redstart	Ac	Ac
Rufous-capped Warbler	Ac	
Yellow-breasted Chat	C - U	C - U
Hepatic Tanager	R	FC - U
Summer Tanager	C - U	C - U
Scarlet Tanager	Ca	Ca
Western Tanager	FC	C - U (L)
Flame-colored Tanager	Ac	
Olive Sparrow	R (ir)	
Green-tailed Towhee	FC	R
Eastern Towhee	Ac	
Spotted Towhee	C - U	C - FC
Canyon Towhee	Ab - FC	Ab - FC
Botteri's Sparrow		Ac
Cassin's Sparrow	FC	FC
Rufous-crowned Sparrow	C - FC	C - FC
American Tree Sparrow		
Chipping Sparrow	Ab - C	Ab - C (L)
Clay-colored Sparrow	U - R	
Brewer's Sparrow	C - U	
Field Sparrow	U - R	
Black-chinned Sparrow	U	C (L)
Vesper Sparrow	FC - U	
Lark Sparrow	C - U	C - U
Black-throated Sparrow	Ab - C	Ab - C
Sage Sparrow		

FALL	WINTER	NESTS	MOST OFTEN OBSERVED	REVIEW SPECIES
Ac				
Ca				X
Ca	x (L)	BB		
				X
Ac	Ac			X
C - U		x	RG	
R	Ac	x	MT	
U		x		
FC	Ac	x (L)	GU	
				X
			VA (ab)	
FC	FC	x (L)		
C - U	C - U	x	MT	
Ab - FC	Ab - FC	x		
		x (L)		
FC - U	U (L)	x		
C - FC	C - FC	x	MT	
	Ca			
Ab - C	Ab - C	x	MT	
FC - U	R			
C - U	C - U			
U - R	U - R			
U	U	x (L)	MT (ab)	
FC - U	U			
C - U	U - R	x		
Ab - C	Ab - C	x		
	U (L) (ir)		NO (ab)	

BIRDS OF THE TRANS-PECOS	SPRING	SUMMER
Lark Bunting	C - FC	U - R
Savannah Sparrow	C - U	
Baird's Sparrow	R (L)	
Grasshopper Sparrow	U - Ca (ir)	R - (L)
LeConte's Sparrow	Ca	
Nelson's Sharp-tailed Sparrow		
Fox Sparrow	R	
Song Sparrow	C - U	
Lincoln's Sparrow	C - FC	
Swamp Sparrow	FC - U	
White-throated Sparrow	U - R	
Harris's Sparrow		
White-crowned Sparrow	Ab - C	
Golden-crowned Sparrow	Ca	
Dark-eyed Junco	C - FC	
Yellow-eyed Junco	Ca	Ca
McCown's Longspur		
Lapland Longspur		
Smith's Longspur	Ac	
Chestnut-collared Longspur	Ca	
Snow Bunting	Ac	
Northern Cardinal	FC - R	FC - R
Pyrrhuloxia	C	C - U
Rose-breasted Grosbeak	R	
Black-headed Grosbeak	FC - U	C
Blue Grosbeak	C	C
Lazuli Bunting	FC - R	
Indigo Bunting	R	R
Varied Bunting	FC - U	FC - U

FALL	WINTER	NESTS	MOST OFTEN OBSERVED	REVIEW SPECIES
C - FC	C - FC	x (L) (ir)		
C - U	C - U			
R (L)	R (L)		(ab)	X
U - Ca (ir)	U -Ca (ir)	x (L)		
Ca	Ca			
	Ac			
R	R			
C - U	C - U		NO	
C - FC	C - FC			
FC - U	FC - U			
U - R	U - R			
	Ca			
C	Ab - C			
Ca	Ca			X
FC - U	C - FC	x (L)		
	Ca		MT	X
Ca	R		NO	
	Ac		NO	
	Ac			
U - R	U - R			
	Ac			X
FC - R	FC - R	x	VA	
C - U	C	x		
Ca				
FC - U		x	MT	
C	Ca	x		
FC - R	Ac			
R		x (L) (ir)	RG	
FC - U	Ca	x	BB (ab)	

BIRDS OF THE TRANS-PECOS	SPRING	SUMMER
Painted Bunting	C - U	C - U
Dickcissel	Ac	Ca
Bobolink	Ac	
Red-winged Blackbird	C - FC	C - FC
Eastern Meadowlark	U	U
Western Meadowlark	C - FC	C - FC
Yellow-headed Blackbird	FC - R	R
Rusty Blackbird		
Brewer's Blackbird	Ab - C	Ca (ir)
Common Grackle	U - R	U (L)
Great-tailed Grackle	Ab (L)	Ab (L)
Bronzed Cowbird	FC - R	FC - R
Brown-headed Cowbird	C	C
Black-vented Oriole	Ac	Ac
Orchard Oriole	C - U	C - U
Hooded Oriole	FC - R (L)	FC - R (L)
Baltimore Oriole	Ca	
Bullock's Oriole	FC - U	FC - U
Scott's Oriole	C	C
Purple Finch	Ac	
Cassin's Finch	U (L)	Ca (L)
House Finch	Ab - C	Ab - C
Red Crossbill	FC - U (L)	FC - U (L)
Pine Siskin	C - FC	R
Lesser Goldfinch	C - FC	C - R
Lawrence's Goldfinch		
American Goldfinch	FC - U	
Evening Grosbeak	R	
House Sparrow	Ab - C	Ab - C

FALL	WINTER	NESTS	MOST OFTEN OBSERVED	REVIEW SPECIES
C - U		x (L)	RG	
R - U (ir)		x? (L) (ir)		
C - FC	C - FC	x		
U	U	x (L)		
C - FC	C - FC	x		
FC - R	FC - R	x (H)		
	Ca			
Ab - C	Ab - C	x (H)		
U - R	U - R	x (L)	(ab)	
Ab (L)	Ab (L)	x (L)		
FC - R		x	BB	
C	U - R	x		
				X
C - U		x	BB	
U (L)		x (L)	BB (ab)	
Ca				
FC - U	Ca	x (L)		
U	Ca	x	BB (ab)	
	Ac			
R (L)	U (L)		GU (ab)	
Ab - C	Ab - C	x		
FC - U (L)	FC - U (L)	x (L) (ir)	GU	
C - FC	C - FC	x (H)		
C - FC	U	x		
Ca	Ca			X
FC - U	FC - U			
	R		GU	
Ab - C	Ab - C	x		

SPECIES OF SPECIAL INTEREST

Clark's Grebe *(Podiceps clarkii)*

Regularly seen at Lake Balmorhea and McNary Reservoir in fall and winter. Nesting birds in spring and summer are not as conspicuous. Irregular at other large lakes and reservoirs.

Common Black-Hawk *(Buteogallus anthracinus)*

Seen regularly in season near the town of Fort Davis. Birds have nested for many years along Limpia Creek near the junction of Highways 118 and 17. The creek itself is on fenced private property, and there is no trespassing, but birds will occasionally fly over the highway.

Gray Hawk *(Asturina nitida)*

Not regular every summer, but cottonwood groves along the Rio Grande would be the preferred habitat. Most sightings are from Brewster County.

Zone-tailed Hawk *(Buteo albonotatus)*

Nests regularly in the central and southern Trans-Pecos at high elevations, but not commonly observed. Sometimes seen along cliffs or in mountain canyons. Occasionally seen at lower elevations outside of breeding season, where it has been known to soar with Turkey Vultures.

Golden Eagle *(Aquila chrysaetos)*

Observed most regularly during fall and winter in mountains, foothills, and grasslands. The Guadalupe Mountains, Franklin Mountains, Chisos Mountains, and several smaller mountain ranges have regular wintering birds. Although Golden Eagles regularly nest in the Trans-Pecos, they are not as commonly seen during breeding season.

Montezuma Quail *(Cyrtonyx montezumae)*

The best spot to view this species is at Davis Mountains State Park early in the mornings or late in the afternoon. Occasionally these birds come down from the surrounding hills to feed at campsites. Individuals should inquire about viewing opportunities at the park headquarters. Montezuma Quail frequent the high grasslands around much of the Davis Mountains area but are not prone to take flight and are not easily observed.

Gambel's Quail *(Callipepla gambelii)*

Observed most often along the Rio Grande north of Presidio County or in brushy washes in western Hudspeth and El Paso counties. Uncommon but regular at Hueco Tanks State Park.

Mountain Plover *(Charadrius montanus)*

This species has nested regularly in the Davis Mountains on private property, but this isolated nesting population appears to be declining. Birds prefer short-grass fields with patches of bare ground for nesting.

Band-tailed Pigeon *(Columba fasciata)*

Most often observed April–October above 5,000 ft. in the Davis and Chisos mountains. At times it is shy and difficult to see, and it is most often observed away from populated areas. This bird can be observed in and around Davis Mountains State Park or on a hike above the Basin Campground in Big Bend National Park.

Flammulated Owl *(Otus flammeolus)*

Usually seen or heard early in the breeding season within the high coniferous forest of the major mountain ranges. More common in the Guadalupe Mountains. Hiking and camping are usually required to gain access to these remote areas in the Guadalupe and Chisos mountains. There is no public park habitat at that elevation in the Davis Mountains.

Western Screech-Owl *(Otus kennicottii)*

Both species of screech-owl nest in the southern Trans-Pecos. However, Western Screech-Owls are easily identified by voice when calling (generally March–June). They can be observed in a variety of habitats including low-elevation mesquite thickets, cottonwood galleries, riparian areas, and higher canyons. They nest up to around 5,500 ft. and are found at that elevation most frequently in the Chisos and Davis mountains (including Davis Mountains State Park). This bird becomes somewhat rare and local in the northwestern Trans-Pecos.

Black-tailed Gnatcatcher

Elf Owl *(Micrathene whitneyi)*

Most often observed at Big Bend National Park in Rio Grande Village Campground or, less commonly, at Cottonwood Campground. In spring, birds regularly call when it becomes dark after 9:00 p.m.

Lucifer Hummingbird *(Calothorax lucifer)*

This species is largely a Big Bend specialty. It is rare but regular around the Davis Mountains. It is seen most often in foothill canyons and arroyos of Big Bend National Park during breeding season, with more observations from late summer after birds begin to wander. It is occasionally seen at feeders but always outnumbered there by competing Black-chinneds.

Thick-billed Kingbird *(Tyrannus crassirostris)*

Although this species has nested at various times in Big Bend National Park, it should not be considered regular. Its most recent string of nesting (1988–1991) occurred in cottonwood trees in Cottonwood Campground, Big Bend National Park.

Black-capped Vireo *(Vireo atricapillus)*

This species is much more easily observed on the Edwards Plateau east of the Trans-Pecos. However, this bird does nest along the Devils River in Val Verde County. Scattered nesting exists elsewhere in the southern Trans-Pecos counties, with a few birds nesting in the Chisos Mountains of Big Bend. No records from the northern Trans-Pecos.

Gray Vireo *(Vireo vicinior)*

Gray Vireos are thinly scattered throughout the Trans-Pecos. They are seen in spring and summer along the Devils River in Val Verde County, McKittrick Canyon in Guadalupe Mountains National Park, Blue Creek Canyon and Window Trail in Big Bend National Park, and at remote localities elsewhere. They have been observed with some regularity at the Sheffield rest stop near Fort Lancaster State Historical Park on Hwy. 290 in Crockett County, a few miles east of the Pecos River close to the Pecos County border.

Mexican Jay *(Aphelocoma ultramarina)*

Found only above 4,500 ft. in the Chisos Mountains. Sometimes observed on the perimeter of the Basin Campground or along one of the many trails in the Chisos Mountains.

Juniper Titmouse *(Baeolophus ridgwayi)*

In Texas, this bird is observed exclusively in the foothills of Guadalupe Mountains National Park. It is often seen on the eastern side of the park at Pine Springs Campground in oak-juniper habitat.

Black-tailed Gnatcatcher *(Polioptila melanura)*

Most common in southern Brewster, southern and western Presidio, and southeastern Hudspeth counties. It is also seen around Devils River State Natural Area. Perhaps most easily found near the Rio Grande in dry shrub, mesquite thickets, low canyons, and washes. This species becomes more uncommon as one moves north from Big Bend country into the grasslands. It is also quite rare in western Hudspeth and El Paso counties.

Crissal Thrasher *(Toxostoma dorsale)*

Not often seen because of its shy nature. This species can be observed, with a little luck, in Big Bend National Park almost anywhere from the Rio Grande to the Basin Campground. However, it is more easily observed in the northwestern Trans-Pecos in dry flats, riverine thickets, and foothills. Although not common at this location, Hueco Tanks State Park may offer the best opportunity for viewing this bird.

Virginia's Warbler *(Vermivora virginiae)*

Most often observed in Guadalupe Mountains National Park during spring and summer. Found occasionally in the foothills but more often in the high-elevation forests. The most accessible viewing may be along McKittrick Canyon Trail on the east side of the park.

Colima Warbler *(Vermivora crissalis)*

In the United States, this bird is seen exclusively in the high Chisos Mountains of Big Bend. This species is most often observed April–June along either the trail to Boot Canyon or the trail to Laguna Meadow, both of which begin just above the Basin Campground. The hike up either trail is arduous and extra water is essential. However, the bird forages in small oaks and is generally not difficult to see when venturing into the appropriate habitat.

Lucy's Warbler *(Vermivora luciae)*

Until the late 1970's, little was known about nesting Lucy's Warblers in the Trans-Pecos. When these birds are not singing, they remain somewhat shy and reclusive in their preferred habitat along the Rio Grande floodplain from Brewster County to eastern Hudspeth County. At Cottonwood Campground in Big Bend National Park, they have nested in dense mesquite thickets north of the adjoining camping area.

Painted Redstart *(Myioborus pictus)*

Found high in the Chisos Mountains in Boot Spring and perhaps best observed right around the spring itself (consider yourself lucky if you actually find water). More often seen in the shade of conifers but not particularly difficult to see when present. A pair was recently discovered nesting in the Davis Mountains on private property, but sightings of this species should not be expected in that mountain range. Numbers fluctuate in the Trans-Pecos from year to year, but even in good years this species is scarce.

Hepatic Tanager *(Piranga flava)*

Found at high elevations in spring and summer, but there is some elevation overlap with the similar (and more common) Summer Tanager. Around the Basin Campground in the Chisos Mountains, for example, both species can occur. As the habitat changes to montane forest above the campground, Hepatic Tanagers become the more dominant of the two species.

Varied Bunting *(Passerina versicolor)*

This bird is somewhat uncommon but still seen regularly throughout the Big Bend country. It has been observed along the Window Trail in the Basin Campground of the Chisos Mountains and in foothill canyons down into the adjoining desert, where it is sometimes observed along dry streambeds. The best chance for observing this species may be at Big Bend Ranch State Park, where it is fairly common.

Black-chinned Sparrow *(Spizella atrogularis)*

A bird of the high grassland and found most often in the major mountain ranges. Seen frequently in tall grasses at Laguna Meadow above the Basin Campground in the Chisos Mountains. Also found around the grasslands of Davis Mountains State Park and along McKittrick Canyon Trail in the Guadalupe Mountains.

Baird's Sparrow *(Ammodramus bairdii)*

Observations of this bird may be increasing, but this may be directly related to the number of capable bird-watchers looking for it. Sometimes found in the high grasslands of the Davis Mountains, with several sightings along (or just off) Highway 166 west of the town of Fort Davis. Observations range from October to April. Occasionally found in winter or in migration in the Chisos Mountains, but not predictable anywhere. As this is a review species, written details are requested.

Bronzed Cowbird *(Molothrus aeneus)*

This species is now seen regularly from March to October throughout much of the Trans-Pecos. Usually easy to observe around campgrounds in Big Bend National Park or at ranches and farm buildings where livestock gathers.

Hooded Oriole *(Icterus cucullatus)*

Apparently decreasing but still seen regularly in mesquites and cottonwoods at campgrounds in Big Bend National Park. Cottonwood Campground on the west side of the park usually maintains a few nesting birds in spring and summer.

BIBLIOGRAPHY

American Ornithologists' Union. 1983. Checklist of North American birds, 6th ed. Washington, D.C.

Arnold, K. A. 1987. Atlasing handbook. Texas Breeding Bird Atlas Project. Texas A&M University, College Station, Texas.

———. 1995. The T.O.S. checklist of the birds of Texas, 3rd ed. Texas Ornithological Society, Austin, Texas.

Davis, W. A., and S. M. Russell. 1990. Birds in southeastern Arizona, 3rd ed. Tucson Audubon Society, Tucson, Arizona.

Espy, P., and J. Miller. 1972. Birds of Jeff Davis County. Fort Davis, Texas.

Espy, P., and F. Williams. 1991. Birds of the Davis Mountains State Park, a seasonal checklist. Texas Parks and Wildlife Department, Austin, Texas.

Howell, S. N. G., and S. Webb. 1995. A guide to the birds of Mexico and northern Central America. Oxford University Press, New York.

Kutac, E. A. 1993. Birder's guide to Texas, 2nd ed. Gulf Publishing Co., Houston, Texas.

Lasley, G. W., and C. Sexton. 1988a. Fall season, Texas region. American Birds 42(4):456–462.

———. 1988b. Winter season, Texas region. American Birds 42(5): 1310–1315.

———. 1989a. Spring season, Texas region. American Birds 43(1): 127–133.

———.1989b. Summer season, Texas region. American Birds 43 (2): 333–340.

———. 1989c. Fall season, Texas region. American Birds 43(3): 502–510.

———.1989d. Winter season, Texas region. American Birds 43(5): 1337–1342.

———. 1990a. Spring season, Texas region. American Birds 44(1): 118–127.

———. 1990b. Summer season, Texas region. American Birds 44 (2):288–296.

———. 1990c. Fall season, Texas region. American Birds 44(3): 458–465.

———. 1990d. Winter season, Texas region. American Birds 44(5): 1154–1158.

———. 1991a. Spring season, Texas region. American Birds 45(1): 124–129.

———. 1991b. Summer season, Texas region. American Birds 45 (2):290–294.

———. 1991c. Fall season, Texas region. American Birds 45(3): 469–474.

———. 1991d. Christmas counts (1989), Texas. American Birds 45 (4):870–901.

———. 1991e. Winter season, Texas region. American Birds 45(5): 1135–1140.

———. 1992a. Spring season, Texas region. American Birds 46(1): 117–123.

———. 1992b. Summer season, Texas region. American Birds 46 (2):286–290.

———. 1992c. Fall season, Texas region. American Birds 46(3): 446–451.

———. 1992d. Winter season, Texas region. American Birds 46(5): 1154–1160.

———. 1993a. Spring season, Texas region. American Birds 47(1): 115–120.

———. 1993b. Christmas counts (1992), Texas. American Birds 47 (4):836–868.

———. 1994a. Summer season, Texas region. American Birds 48 (2):224–228.

———. 1994b. Fall season, Texas region. American Birds 48(3): 316–322.

———. 1994c. Christmas counts (1993), Texas. American Birds 48 (4):717–750.

———. 1994d. Winter season, Texas region. American Birds 48(5): 960–966.

———. 1995a. Spring season, Texas region. Field Notes 49(1):67–71.

———.1995b. Summer season, Texas region. Field Notes 49(2):164– 170.

———. 1995c. Fall season, Texas region. Field Notes 49(3):273–278.

———. 1995d. Christmas counts (1994), Texas. Field Notes 49(4): 689–721.

———. 1995e. Winter season, Texas region. Field Notes 49(5): 948–954.

———. 1996a. Spring season, Texas region. Field Notes 50(1):77–81.

———. 1996b. Summer season, Texas region. Field Notes 50(2): 189–193.

———. 1996c. Fall season, Texas region. Field Notes 50(3):300–306.

———. 1996d. Christmas counts (1995), Texas. Field Notes 50(4): 715–746.

———. 1996e. Winter season, Texas region. Field Notes 50(5): 969–973.

LBJ School of Public Affairs, Office of Research. 1973. Mount Livermore and Sawtooth Mountain, a natural area survey: parts III and IV (Ornithology section by J. F. Scudday). University of Texas, Austin.

Lockwood, Mark. 1992. Birds of Balmorhea State Park. Texas Parks and Wildlife, Austin, Texas.

National Geographic Society. 1987. A field guide to the birds of North America, 2nd ed. Washington, D.C.

Newman, G. A. 1975. Compositional aspects of breeding avifaunas in selected woodlands of the southern Guadalupe Mountains, Texas. Pages 181–237 in Biological investigations in the Guadalupe Mountains National Park, Texas (H. H. Genoways and R. J. Baker, Eds.). Proceedings and Transactions Series, no. 4. National Park Service, Washington, D.C.

Oberholser, H. C., and E. B. Kincaid. 1974. The bird life of Texas. University of Texas Press, Austin.

Peterson, J., G. W. Lasley, K. B. Bryan, M. Lockwood. 1991. Additions to the breeding avifauna of the Davis Mountains. Bulletin of the Texas Ornithological Society 24(2):39–48.

Peterson, Roger Tory. 1990. Western birds. Houghton-Mifflin, Boston, Massachusetts.

Popper, D. M. 1951. Notes on the birds of Mt. Locke, Texas. Condor 57:154–178.

Powell, A. M. 1988. Trees and shrubs of Trans-Pecos Texas. Big Bend Natural History Association Inc., Big Bend National Park, Texas.

———. 1994. Grasses of the Trans-Pecos and adjacent areas. University of Texas Press, Austin.

Sibley, C. G., and B. L. Monroe, Jr. 1990. Distribution and taxonomy of birds of the world. Yale University Press, New Haven, Connecticut.

Wauer, R. H. 1996. A field guide to birds of the Big Bend, 2nd ed. Gulf Publishing Co., Houston, Texas.

———. 1998. Birding Texas. Falcon Press, Helena, Montana.

———, and J. D. Ligon. 1974. Distributional relations of breeding avifauna of four southwestern mountain ranges. Pages 567–578 *in* Transactions of the symposium on the biological resources of the Chihuahuan desert region, United States and Mexico (R. Wauer and D. Riskind, Eds.). Proceedings and Transactions Series, no. 3. National Park Service, Washington, D.C.

Weidenfeld, S. 1989. Birds of Seminole Canyon State Park. Texas Parks and Wildlife, Austin, Texas.

Williams, F. 1987a. Fall season, southern Great Plains region. American Birds 41(3):454–458.

———. 1987b. Winter season, southern Great Plains region. American Birds 41(5):1455–1458.

———. 1988a. Spring season, southern Great Plains region. American Birds 42(1):96–100.

———. 1988b. Summer season, southern Great Plains region. American Birds 42(2):282–286.

Zimmer, B. R. 1990. Birds of Hueco Tanks State Historical Park. Texas Parks and Wildlife, Austin, Texas.

———. 1996. Birds of Franklin Mountains State Park. Texas Parks and Wildlife, Austin, Texas.

INDEX